Uncoverings 1998

Volume 19 of the Research Papers of the
American Quilt Study Group

Edited by Virginia Gunn

Carol Reiman

Published by the American Quilt Study Group
35th and Holdredge Street
Lincoln, Nebraska 68504-0737

Manufactured in the United States.

Uncoverings is indexed in:
America: History and Life
ARTbibliographies
BHA (Bibliography of the History of Art)
Clothing and Textile Arts Index
Feminist Periodicals
Historical Abstracts
MLA International Bibliography
Sociological Abstracts

ISBN 1-877859-14-1
ISSN 0277-0028
Library of Congress catalog number: 81-649486

Cover: Velvet Crazy Quilt, embroidered 1912, 64" x 42"
made by Ida Stover Eisenhower.
Courtesy of the Dwight D. Eisenhower Museum, Abilene, Kansas

Cover photograph by R. G. Elmore
Color separations donated by Arizona Lithographers.

Contents

Preface

The nineteenth seminar of the American Quilt Study Group will be held in Charleston, West Virginia, from October 16-18, 1999. Participants will hear and discuss the research papers presented in this volume, part of an ongoing series dedicated to preserving quilt history. Dr. Alan Jabbour, director of the American Folklife Center at the Library of Congress, will give the invited keynote address, focusing on the Center and developments in quilt documentation and research on the World Wide Web.

While topics related to quilts and technology dominate discussion in quilt-related conversations and concerns in the late 1990s, the papers in this volume have their central focus on the people who make quilts. This is probably as it should be. While the internet and related technologies are changing the way we share information and do research, the heart of quiltmaking is still the quiltmakers themselves and their relationships with families, friends, and extended communities.

Carol and Ronnie Elmore's study of the surviving quilts made by Ida Stover Eisenhower, mother of Dwight David Eisenhower, is a pioneer in-depth exploration of textiles related to presidents. Since objects with associational value have usually been among the first items to interest the museum world, it is surprising this has not happened sooner. Their study reinforces the fact that in the United States extraordinary leaders often grew up in quite ordinary circumstances where creative and caring people made a key difference in their lives.

Dorothy Osler's paper reinforces the importance of continued in-depth work on known topics. She builds on her own previous work and that of other British quilt researchers to shed new light on an important quilt design trade which was a long-standing tradition in the North East region of England. She conducted oral interviews, analyzed extant textiles, and mined the printed sources to piece together this fascinating story of professional quilting designers. It adds to our knowledge of women's work and cottage industries as an international phenomenon.

Tracy Barron discovered an amazing quilt preserved in a family collection in Massachusetts. As a teacher of reading, she wanted to decode the messages written on this textile object and in the accompanying papers that had been preserved with it. She uncovered the tale of an interesting nineteenth-century woman and her support circle of friends, family, and mentors. This material-culture approach demonstrates how in-depth study of an artifact may reveal the culture in which the artifact was produced.

Heather Lenz's study of her grandmother's quilts provides us with a rich background on the whole process of quiltmaking as it integrates with life. Heather's interest in the artifacts led her to spend long hours with her grandmother in order to understand and to learn the process of quiltmaking. Heather wisely and instinctively settled on the best way to really understand process as well as product. Formally, this in-depth method would be called field work. The results allow us to share the folk wisdom of her grandmother Mary Sibley.

Judy Elsley's study of quilt detective novels should delight the numerous readers of this genre of literature. She helps us understand why this form of literature is so addictive and relaxing to read. With her training and experience in teaching English literature and with her interest in the place of quilts in contemporary culture, she is able to explain why quilts make a perfect vehicle for modern detective stories which have women as protagonists.

Jenny Yearous's work on the history of thread completes this nineteenth volume of *Uncoverings.* Jenny's study introduces an important topic and points out the need for more in-depth work on the materials and technology related to quilts. Her analysis of quilts in private collections and in the James Collection at the University of Nebraska led her to question published information on the dates that types of thread appeared, and suggested new guidelines. Her study reminds us that research is a continual process of discovery and revision.

The Life and Quilts
of Ida Stover Eisenhower

Carol H. Elmore and Ronnie G. Elmore

Ida Elizabeth Stover Eisenhower (1862–1946), mother of Dwight D. Eisenhower, the thirty-fourth president of the United States, made quilts while an orphan in Virginia; a young transient in Hope, Kansas, and Denison, Texas; and a struggling housewife with six robust boys living on the "wrong side" of the tracks in Abilene, Kansas. Twenty-three quilts and five quilted pillow tops have survived the many years of use by the Eisenhower family. Original research at the Eisenhower Center in Abilene, Kansas, and the Ida Eisenhower birthplace near Mount Sidney, Virginia, and an extensive literature search support the conclusion that Ida developed a quilting style of her own that included elements of improvisation, asymmetry, and multiple-patterning. Ida found making quilts a creative and pleasurable diversion from her challenging daily life.

Although no one knows how many quilted pieces Ida Stover Eisenhower, mother of the thirty-fourth president of the United States, made during her lifetime, twenty-seven quilts, tops, and pillows are housed at the Eisenhower Center in Abilene, Kansas, and one quilt is kept at the Dwight D. Eisenhower birthplace in Denison, Texas (see appendix). These quilts represent all of the periods of Ida's life from 1862 until 1946: her years as a young girl in Virginia; as a college girl and young housewife in Lecompton and Hope, Kansas; as a transient young mother in Denison, Texas; and as a homemaker in Abilene, Kansas.

Ida considered sewing a reward for carefully managing the many chores incumbent in raising a large family on the developing prairie. During an extended interview recorded in 1943, Ida Eisenhower indicated that after all of the mending, darning, and clothing manufacture—and of course, daily cooking and weekly laundry and cleaning were out of the way—only then, had she "earned a right to do fancywork!"[1] Ida talked about making quilts—"the common kind, made from squares of wool from cast-off clothing, and fancy ones of cretonne and silkaline. With all of the goods in one piece, you could tie a fancy comfort in an afternoon, and sometimes took weeks piecing out others."[2]

Although Ida Eisenhower's quilts probably would not be considered to be exceptional by today's standards, they are important because they were made by an unsung heroine who raised six very successful sons, one a president of the United States.[3] Ida lived and made quilts during extremely difficult times—during the period of reconstruction in Virginia after the Civil War and during the turbulent development of Kansas, then the eastern edge of the wild West. Ida's quilts are the products of a wife and mother of a very traditional working family with a meager income living during the late nineteenth and first half of the twentieth centuries. Ida Eisenhower's inclusion of elements of improvisation, asymmetry, and multiple-patterning in her quilts are in stark contrast to her very routine, ordinary life. Ida demonstrated her creative talents through her quiltmaking.

Mount Sidney, Virginia
May 1, 1862–1883
Age: birth to 21

Ida Elizabeth Stover was born to Simon P. and Elizabeth J.(I.)Stover in Augusta County in western Virginia, on May 1, 1862, in a picturesque farm house located on a narrow road winding uphill from the little hamlet of Mount Sidney.[4] The Stovers had settled in Augusta County sometime between the years 1727 and 1732. Here they had lived through the American Revolution, the War of 1812, the Mexican War, the Spanish-American War, and now the Civil War. Although pictures and descriptions of Ida Stover's birthplace give the impression of a pleasant pastoral setting—a two-story farm house on a hillside surrounded by fertile acres of farmland, blooming orchards, and stately trees—it must be remembered that not far away in the Shenandoah Valley in the foothills of the Blue Ridge Mountains, Union and Confederate troops were battling. Ida was only three years old when the Civil War ended. Its horrors, however, left a deep impression on her. Her family's very strong religious convictions of pacifism and opposition to slavery had caused them to be distrusted by many of their Southern neighbors. Ida stated in later life that the stress of the Civil War caused the early death of her mother. In the 1943 interview, just three years before her death, Ida remembered: "Raiding soldiers, coming through, worrying my mother, frightening her till she died of it! It's all a kind of horror, still. I hated war, with all my soul. Then my father—gone, too. It was like being pulled up by the roots. To be taken off by relatives!"[5]

Five-year-old Ida Stover had seven brothers ranging in age from three to seventeen when her mother died. Ida's father could not handle his large family and the reconstruction of his war-torn farm alone and, therefore, sent his children a few miles up the road to live with their maternal grandparents in 1867. After a couple of years Ida was sent to live with a maternal uncle, Billy Link. Five years later, when Ida was twelve, her father died and Uncle Billy became her legal guardian.

Ida Stover's memories of growing up in her relatives' homes reflected a rather unhappy childhood. "Because I was a girl," Ida Eisenhower remarked nearly eighty years later, "I was told I must listen, not talk, and not expect to go to school much." Instead she was expected to do most of the cooking for her brothers. There was a big brick oven; this became her nemesis: "If I burned anything or took it out underdone, I was punished."[6]

Francis T. Miller, Dwight Eisenhower's biographer, noted:

> When Ida was not at school, or cooking meals at home she was generally found in the bare room upstairs making quilts. They were always making quilts. That was the winter pastime. There was no heat in the room and her fingers would get so cold that she would often botch the work and then have to pull it all out and do it over again. It seemed that they were keeping everlasting at it. If you could cook and quilt that was about all a girl had a right to know.[7]

Figure 1. Candlewick bedspread made and signed by Ida Stover.
Photograph by R. G. Elmore.

After her interview with Ida in 1943, Kunigunde Duncan wrote:

> a clear picture (developed) of a heartsore little Ida, climbing the steep
> stairs alone in the quilting room of her relatives, there to do her allot-
> ted daily stint–and pull it out and put it in over, out and over, as many
> times as commanded, and in silence. At ten she had been an expert at
> darning, patching, hemming.[8]

The earliest known bedcover made by Ida Stover still in existence is a 91" by 67" candlewick bedspread (see figure 1). The design on this spread was created by hooking cotton roving through
a single layer of white cotton fabric. The design features a flower
basket in the center and a vine border on the left side and across
the bottom. The spread is boldly signed in big letters: "Ida Stover." Because of the signature it is assumed that this spread was
made while Ida was still a child living in Virginia.

Although Ida Stover had much to be sad about as a young girl,
her friends remembered her as "a very pretty girl with light hair,

very vivacious and attractive, and indeed quite charming." One friend noted that Ida was a bright student and very popular.[9] She apparently was the life of the parties held at each other's homes and attended the nearby Salem Lutheran Church, where she was quite active. Others who knew Ida as a child provided the following composite picture of her: "A fun loving, light-haired, vivacious, attractive girl who did well in her studies, but was something of a tom-boy. She also was devout, eager for an education, and particularly interested in music."[10]

Occasionally, Ida was allowed to ride horses with her brothers into the neighboring woods where the orphaned children discussed their futures. Since each of the children would receive a small inheritance as they reached legal age, these plans could become more than just wishful thoughts. Apparently the children decided that when they were adults they would seek their fortunes in far away Kansas. For Ida this would not be an idle dream.

In the latter years of her life Ida vividly remembered the time she had spent in the quilting room of her relatives' home in Virginia.[11] It is probable that Ida made her Wandering Foot quilt during this time for her hope chest and eventually took it with her to Kansas.[12] During Ida's latter years the quilt was kept on a shelf in a make-shift closet with a white sheet hanging on the front in the southwest bedroom on the second floor of the Eisenhower home in Abilene, Kansas.

Ida's rose and blue Wandering Foot quilt has lost much of its original brightness. The cotton fabric is yellowed and very worn with many areas of severe fabric deterioration which have been covered with netting for stabilization.[13] The quilt has a muslin backing which is turned to the front as binding. It is hand pieced and hand quilted in parallel lines using 8–9 stitches per inch.

During her youth Ida Stover also made a hand-pieced, hand-quilted, solid green-and-white cotton quilt in a Six-Pointed Star with Hexagons (Tumbling Block) pattern (see figure 3). The backing on this quilt is white muslin.

Another of Ida Stover's earliest pieces is a bright red, brown, and black wool quilt in an Eight-Pointed Star (Evening Star) pattern (see figure 4). The quilt has a striped flannel backing which is turned to the front as binding. The quilt is hand pieced and loosely hand quilted with four stitches per inch. Although the stitches are

Figure 2. Wandering Foot quilt (Turkey Tracks), ca. 1875, made by Ida Stover while a teenager in Virginia. Photograph by R. G. Elmore.

very course, the rich colors make this a very visually striking quilt. Ida's early quilts clearly demonstrate that she learned the traditional ways of quiltmaking during her youth.

Ida ran away from her uncle's home to the county seat in Staunton when she was about fifteen years old. She had no difficulty finding a family willing to give her room and board in exchange

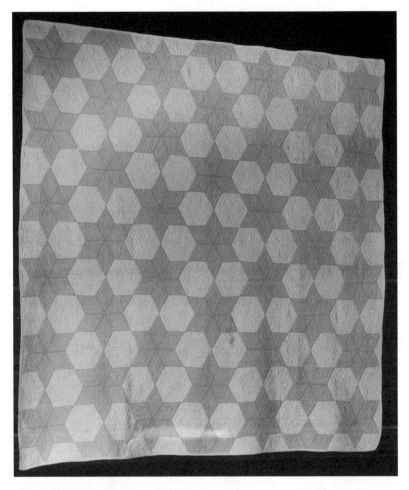

Figure 3. Six-Pointed Star with Hexagons (Tumbling Block), ca. 1875, quilt made by Ida Stover while a teenager in Virginia. Photograph courtesy of Dwight D. Eisenhower Library.

for cooking and helping with the daily chores. Here Ida attended high school. After graduation she got a job teaching in a country school. She was waiting to reach the magical age of twenty-one, when she could claim her inheritance and escape the oppression she felt as a young orphan girl.

Figure 4. Eight-Pointed Star (Evening Star), ca. 1875, wool quilt made by Ida Stover while a teenager in Virginia. Photograph courtesy of Dwight D. Eisenhower Library.

LeCompton, Kansas
1883–1885
Age: 21–23

While she was still a child, two of Ida Eisenhower's brothers made their way to Kansas. Because of their excitement about living in the wild West, Ida decided to move west too. During the summer of 1883, with her small inheritance, Ida arrived in Topeka, Kansas. She soon enrolled in Lane University, a small college sponsored by the United Brethren church in LeCompton, Kansas. At this time higher education for women was considered improper in Virginia and, further, Ida defied her River Brethren tradition to gain a college education. Ida eagerly studied music, history, and English.

Classmates soon noticed Ida. Apparently there was intense competition among the male students of Lane University for dates with Ida. David Eisenhower, a shy, thoughtful young engineering student from Hope, Kansas, made winning Ida his primary goal. By the end of his sophomore year David abandoned his plans to become an engineer and turned his full attention to Ida. The young couple complemented each other quite well—she was vivacious and outgoing while he was quite introverted. Many years later while reminiscing about Lane, Ida remembered David as "so much quieter than most, and fastidious in dress and in what he did and said."[14]

There is no evidence that Ida Stover made quilts while a busy college student enrolled at Lane University, but while there she did make a decision that changed the direction of her life, and ultimately, had an impact on world history. During the spring term of 1885, David and Ida were engaged and they married on his birthday, September 23, 1885, in the university chapel (see figure 5).[15] Following their marriage David and Ida decided not to return to Lane University to complete their degrees. Instead they moved to Hope, Kansas, to start a business and a family.

Figure 5. David and Ida Stover Eisenhower's wedding picture, taken on September 23, 1885, at Lane University in LeCompton, Kansas. Photograph courtesy of Dwight D. Eisenhower Library.

Hope, Kansas
1885–1889
Age: 23–27

Recognizing the necessity of going to work to support his new wife, David Eisenhower returned to Hope, Kansas, to open a general mercantile store on March 30, 1885.[16] His partner, also recently wed, was Milton D. Good.[17] Good had been clerking in an Abilene clothing store (see figure 6).[18] To get the new store started Milton furnished the business experience and David provided most of the capital from his father's wedding gift, a quarter section of prime Kansas farm land and two thousand dollars. The store was housed in a two-story building with two small apartments on the second floor, one for the Goods and one for the Eisenhowers (see figure 7).[19]

The Good and Eisenhower store flourished during the first two years of its existence (see figure 8). Soon, however, droughts and grasshoppers caused many of their customers to lose income.[20] The young businessmen had to extend more and more credit and it soon became necessary for David to borrow money to keep the store operating.[21]

It is an understatement to say that David paid less attention to the books of his store than he should have. He turned most of his assets over to his partner to pay bills and wrongfully assumed that the store's books were balancing. Sometime during the fall of 1888, Milton Good and his family left Hope unexpectedly. David soon discovered that many of the bills that he thought had been paid were still outstanding. David quickly turned everything over to a local lawyer and accepted the first job he could find–a low-paying job as an engine wiper for the Missouri, Kansas and Texas Railroad, also known as the Katy, in Denison, Texas. After David left Hope the store was sold and every available asset was used to pay off his creditors.

Ida Eisenhower stayed in Hope to right the situation. She was convinced that their partner had robbed them and that their lawyer was also charging them exorbitant fees. Now pregnant for the second time, Ida borrowed some law books to study, hoping that she could regain some of their assets. In the end all she managed

Figure 6. Milton D. Good with his daughter, Rose, on the left and his sister-in-law, Eva Gleissner, in the center (1912). Rose later became Rose Kretsinger. Photograph courtesy of Kansas State Historical Society.

Figure 7. Civil War reunion picture in front of the Good and Eisenhower Store, ca. 1885, in Hope, Kansas. The Eisenhowers and Goods lived in apartments above the store. Photograph courtesy of Dwight D. Eisenhower Library.

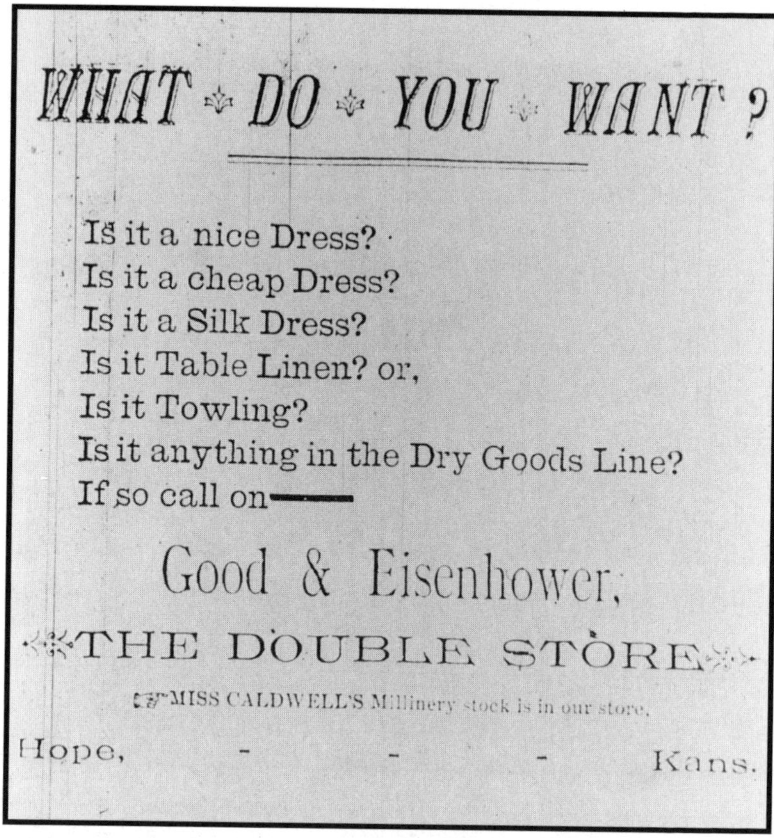

Figure 8. Advertisement from *Hope Herald*, 20 May 1886, 2. Photograph by R. G. Elmore.

to keep were a few pieces of furniture, including her prized piano. In spite of all of their difficulties in Hope, Ida, many years later remembered, "Hope was such a nice little town."[22]

Shortly after the birth of Edgar, Ida and her two very young boys went to join David in Texas. Ida later recalled, "I was as frightened as at any time in my life, when I started out alone, for Texas, a toddler at my skirts and a month-old baby in my arms."[23]

Although it is unknown whether Ida made any quilts while living in Hope, it is likely that some of the fabrics that she eventually used in her later quilts were goods from the Good and Eisenhower mercantile store.

Denison, Texas
1889–1891
Age: 27–29

The two years that the Eisenhowers lived in Texas were very unhappy ones. David's salary was less than forty dollars per month
and they were separated from their family and friends. During these
difficult years in Texas Ida gave birth to a third son, David Dwight
(later changed to Dwight David).[4]

The years in Texas were particularly difficult for Ida's husband,
David. Apparently the chief source of David's strength at that time,
as in later life, was Ida. She had the kind of vivid, intense personality which energized those around her. She took full responsibility
for managing the house and caring for the children. She maintained,
at least outwardly, a bright, cheerful optimism through most of the
dark hours; and whether consciously or unconsciously, she managed to help David restore his badly damaged self-confidence. Ida
became, in everything but name, the head of the family. She did it,
however, in such a way as to stimulate rather than destroy her
husband's self-respect.[24]

It is likely, that Ida, amidst all of the hardships, made some quilts
while living in Texas. Many years after moving to Washington to
practice law, her son, Edgar said, "I remember too helping mother
sew small patches of cloth together to make bed quilts. You just
don't see bed covers like that anymore."[25]

Currently displayed in the Texas home is a Tumbling Blocks
pattern quilt, said to be a quilt Ida made. A 1989 newspaper article
referred to this quilt as a Jacob's Ladder design and stated that Ida
enlisted the help of two of her small sons to cut out the pieces for
the quilt and help fit them together.[26] The article identified the two
sons as Dwight and Milton.[27] Since Dwight was less than two years
old and Milton had not yet been born, the newspaper account is
not completely accurate. It is more likely that Arthur and Edgar
helped their mother make this quilt, if it was actually made in
Denison.

Abilene, Kansas
1891–1946
Age: 29–84

Two events prompted the Eisenhower's move to Abilene, Kansas, in 1891–David's mother's death and an offer of a job as an engineer (mechanic) at Belle Springs Creamery. David's father strongly encouraged him to move back to Dickinson County, Kansas, where there were relatives and friends. David and his growing family rented a very small house on Northeast Second Street. Here three more sons (Roy, Paul, and Earl) were born. Paul who was unhealthy from the time of his birth lived for only a few months. Although life was not easy in Abilene at the turn of the century, Ida was extremely pleased to be living among friends and relatives and to retrieve her few stored possessions, including her prized black ebony piano.

In 1898, Dr. Abraham Lincoln Eisenhower, a veterinarian and David's brother, decided to leave Abilene. He sold his simple two-story frame Victorian-era farm cottage, built in 1887, and three acres across the tracks on the south outskirts of town to David. The house on Fourth Street was small by today's standards (818 square feet) for a family of eight plus an elderly parent. Still Dwight Eisenhower noted that the house "seemed a mansion with its upstairs bedrooms."[28] At first Dwight slept with two brothers in one large room on the second floor. His parents and baby brother, Earl, occupied a second bedroom, and the oldest son, Arthur, slept in a very small room at the end of the hall. The first floor of the house contained a front parlor, a back parlor, and a combined dining room and kitchen. Two small bedrooms were soon added to the first floor. The last of the Eisenhower boys, Milton, was born a few months after the family moved to their new home.

Ida Eisenhower lived the rest of her life in the Fourth Street house. She had to be very efficient in doing her endless work. The very large barn on their three acres was always filled with an array of farm animals. During the warm months she tended the large vegetable garden and a large orchard. Ida canned vegetables and fruit and helped her boys peddle the surplus to the much more affluent residents on the north side of the tracks. She enjoyed baking nine loaves of bread every other day for her large family. In addition to all of the necessary daily chores, Ida found time to teach her boys music, cooking, and reading.

According to most accounts, Ida Eisenhower was generally happy throughout her entire life in Abilene. Humming a hymn as she worked, Ida Eisenhower was demonstrably more than merely contented with her lot–like Cinderella, she was living happily ever after, Kansas style (see figure 9).[29] She often commented that "there is no rest for the wicked." Her husband worked very hard too–usually leaving for work at six in the morning and returning at six in the evening.

David and Ida Eisenhower were deeply religious people. After supper David usually sat reading or studying a very large homemade wall-sized diagram of the Egyptian pyramids. He had some abstruse theories about their construction and found satisfaction in trying to prove them. Although the boys always spoke of their parents' marriage as an ideal partnership, it is easy to conclude that David was generally the silent partner. David had a quick temper and was swift to discipline and probably passed his strong work ethic to his sons.

Unlike David, Ida was an easily identifiable influence on her sons. She was constantly with them. Dwight said, "Mother was by far the greatest influence in our lives. She spent many hours a day with us, while father's time with us was largely at supper and in the evening."[30]

David and Ida gave each of their six sons the freedom to develop and go their individual ways. This was particularly difficult when Dwight chose to become a soldier. Ida believed that soldiering was wicked. Although both David and Ida were crushed when Dwight applied to West Point and eventually left to enroll, neither said a word to dissuade him.

When Dwight picked up his suitcase to walk to the Union Pacific depot to begin his journey to West Point in 1911, Ida stood on her front porch and waved to him. Milton, standing beside her, later stated that she did not shed a tear until Dwight disappeared from sight. Then tears flooded down her cheeks and she spent the day alone in her room.[31] Ida, however, was always extremely proud of all her boys and always defended their right to make their own

Figure 9. David Eisenhower family in 1902 when Ida was forty years old. Dwight is the boy on the far left of the picture. Photograph courtesy of Dwight D. Eisenhower Library.

decisions, just as she did as a young woman so many years earlier.[32]

Early in 1942, when he was nearly eighty, David died. Within a short period of time, Ida's grief gave way to a calmness of spirit. At about this time, however, her memory began to seriously fail. She maintained a very cheerful attitude and often joked about her lack of ability to remember anything. Ida's sons hired a practical nurse companion to live with her for the remainder of her life. Ida Eisenhower died quietly in her sleep on September 11, 1946, at the age of eighty-four.

Apparently, Ida Eisenhower made many quilts while living on Fourth Street in Abilene. Near the turn of the century she made several crazy quilts containing a variety of fabrics—silks, cottons, cotton sateens, velvets, velveteens, wools, and flannels. It is likely that some of these were made of goods from the failed Good and Eisenhower store in Hope.

The crazy quilts that Ida Eisenhower made during the early 1900s

Figure 10. Crazy Quilt, ca. 1900. This quilt illustrates Ida Eisenhower's tendency to improvise. Four large crazy blocks compose the lower right corner and two asymmetrical borders compose the left and top of the quilt. Photograph courtesy of Dwight D. Eisenhower Library.

show elements of improvisation and asymmetry (see figure 10). Unlike most traditional crazy quilts in which the entire quilt is composed of randomly shaped pieces in no identifiable blocks or in symmetrically placed crazy patch blocks, Ida made large asymmetrical crazy blocks of varying sizes and then attached them to complete an entire quilt. Figure 10 is an excellent example of Ida's asymmetrical crazy quilts. The quilt in figure 10 contains four large blocks grouped together in one corner and two partial "borders" containing crazy blocks of various sizes. Like most traditionally made crazy quilts, Ida's contained a lot of intricate decorative embroidery around the individual crazy patches.

During the early twentieth century, Ida also made very practical functional quilts. An excellent example is a very nonphotogenic utility quilt made of drab green, gray, brown, and tan cotton and wool fabrics (see appendix, H-82). Several of the squares are pieces cut from trousers. Some of these contain the leg seams. The backing is a blue-and-white cotton ticking and the binding is the back-

Figure 11. Old Maid's Puzzle and Twelve Patch Quilt, ca. 1915. This quilt is an example of Ida's use of multiple patterning. Photograph by R. G. Elmore.

ing turned to the front. The binding varies from 3/4" to 4" in width. The quilt is tied with heavy white utility string. This quilt, as well as others, demonstrate Ida's bent towards being practical and frugal. She used the materials that were readily available to her.

Ida Eisenhower's Old Maid's Puzzle and Twelve Patch quilt, 75" by 75", made in the 1910s, illustrates her characteristic combination of multiple-patterning (see figure 11). This quilt, made of blue, brown, red, and pink cotton-print fabrics, is composed of alternating rows of hand-pieced Twelve Patch blocks and Old Maid's Puzzle blocks. The backing of the quilt, which contains imprints of bed springs, is white muslin. The backing is turned to the front for binding.

During the 1920s and 1930s Ida Eisenhower made quilts using the standard patterns and fabrics of the times; however, she often varied the designs by injecting blocks in colors that did not match the overall pattern or by including blocks that were reversed or different in some way (see figures 12 and 13). Ida's quilts often had borders of varying widths. Ida's later quilts usually included some examples of improvisation, asymmetry, or multiple-patterning.

Ida Eisenhower's Eight-Pointed Star (Evening Star) quilt demonstrates her improvisation and use of asymmetrical color placement in her 1930s quilts (see figure 12). The top seven rows have yellow and orange stars, and the bottom row is composed of four pink stars and one purple star.

Since none of the rooms of Ida's house was large enough to lay out the blocks of a large quilt before attaching them, it is possible that Ida merely sewed blocks together off of a stack of blocks and that the pink and purple blocks just happened to be on bottom of the pile. It is also possible that Ida did not have enough yellow and orange blocks to make the quilt the desired size and, therefore, finished the quilt with other colors. It is also possible, however, that Ida intentionally created unusual placements of color to give her quilts a spark of interest.

Ida Eisenhower used two different prints in making the baskets for her Cherry Basket pattern quilt top(see figure 13). In the final construction of her quilt top she did not arrange the blocks symmetrically according to prints as most quilters likely would have done. The seven baskets across the top and down the right side of the quilt are made of the same fabric and the thirteen baskets on

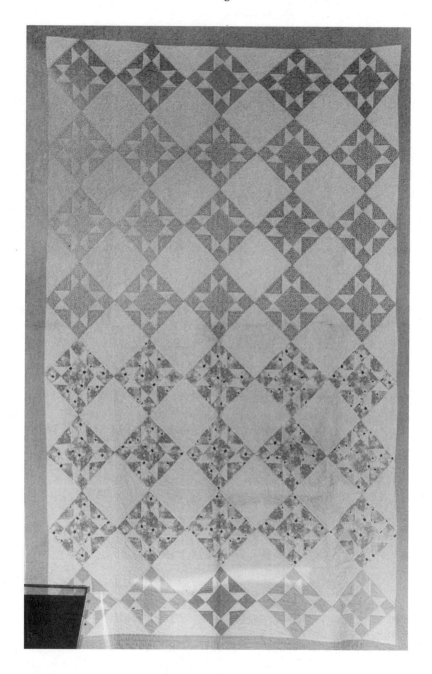

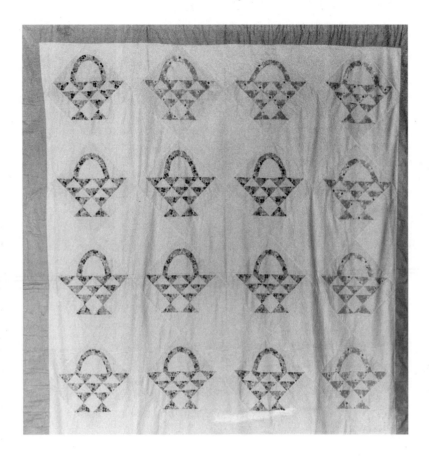

Figure 12. *(Opposite page)* Eight-Pointed Star Quilt (Evening Star), ca. 1930. The top seven rows of this quilt are composed of yellow and orange blocks. The bottom row is composed of four pink blocks and one center purple block. Photograph courtesy of Dwight D. Eisenhower Library.

Figure 13. *(Above)* Cherry Basket Quilt Top, ca. 1935. In this quilt top Ida Eisenhower used two different prints in the baskets. Also, note the unique bases on the baskets. Photograph courtesy of Dwight D. Eisenhower Library.

the lower left of the quilt are made of a different fabric. It is also interesting to note that Ida did not make the bases of her baskets solid as most quilters making this quilt did. It appears that the baskets have feet. Like most Cherry Basket quilts, the handles of the baskets on this quilt are appliqued.

None of the rooms in the Fourth Street house were large enough for Ida Eisenhower to place her quilts in traditional quilting frames. The registrar at the Eisenhower Museum stated that no quilting frames were cataloged after Ida died and said that she had never seen any on the premises. Likewise, several people who recall visiting the Eisenhower home as children have stated that they never saw quilting frames. It is likely that Ida did her quilting in one of the outbuildings or quilted on her lap.

Ida Eisenhower probably quit making quilts during the middle to late 1930s or early 1940s. She suffered from declining health, arthritis, and memory loss. Several of her 1930s pieces are unquilted tops. During an interview in 1943 she asked her interviewer to play her prized piano for her. "Yes," she said, sighing with satisfaction, "I am glad I understand music. Thanks. My hands are too stiff for it now, so I have to depend on folks coming in."[33]

Ida Eisenhower's methods of making quilts may have been dictated by her resources, her limited space to do quilting, her time constraints, or other unknown reasons. It is likely, however, that her strong convictions, keen intellect, and creative talents played important roles in her creation of unusual and interesting quilts.

Ida's quilts reflect her life. Just as a single purple star appears on her quilt of orange and yellow stars, Ida's life stands out because she was able to change the world in spite of having few resources and living among the ordinary. She and David raised six very successful and influential sons on a meager budget during difficult times. Fortunately, the mother of the thirty-fourth president of the United States also felt throughout her busy life that she had "earned the right to sew," and she exercised this "right" by making quilts in her own way.

Acknowledgments

Publication of this paper has been generously supported by gifts from Ronnie Elmore, the Kansas Quilters Organization, and the Professional Appraisers Association of Quilted Textiles (PAAQT).

Notes and References

1. Kunigunde Duncan, *Earning the Right to do Fancy Work*, (Lawrence: University of Kansas Press, 1957), 1–38.
2. Ibid., 20.
3. Doris Faber, *The President's Mother* (New York: St. Martin's Press, 1978), 69, and John McCallum, *Six Roads from Abilene* (Seattle: Wood and Reber, 1960), 112–22. The extremely successful careers of Ida Eisenhower's six sons are strong indicators of her excellent motherly advice and guidance. Arthur was a banker; Edgar was an attorney; Dwight was an army general and thirty-fourth president of the United States; Roy was a pharmacist; Earl was an electrical engineer; and Milton was president of three major universities, including Kansas State University (the first co-educational land-grant university), Pennsylvania State College, and Johns Hopkins University. There were no "black sheep" in the David and Ida Eisenhower family.
4. Kunigunde Duncan, in her book *Earning the Right to do Fancy Work*, lists Ida's mother's name as Elizabeth Ida Stover. She further stated that Ida Elizabeth was named for her mother, but to avoid confusion, her mother's given names were reversed. It is also interesting to note that Dwight David Eisenhower was originally named "David Dwight Eisenhower" after his father. The younger David changed his name to Dwight David to avoid confusion. The original birth records for Ida did not contain her name. Apparently she was not named at the time of her birth.
5. Duncan, 4.
6. Faber, 68.
7. Francis T. Miller, *Eisenhower, Man and Soldier* (Philadelphia: The John C. Winston Company, 1944), 90.
8. Duncan, 17–18.
9. Miller, 22. This was a quote from John W. Wine, a childhood friend of Ida Stover. After Ida left Virginia he bought the house in which she was born. The house is currently owned privately and used as rental property.
10. Ibid.
11. Duncan, 17–18.
12. Quilts made in the Wandering Foot pattern date from the early 1800s. Since this pattern name was thought to convey a sense of wanderlust it was never used on a young person's bed during the westward expansion of the United States for fear that he or she might decide to travel west and never be heard from again. To change this jinx, the name of the pattern was later changed to Turkey Tracks.
13. Conservation procedures were performed on Ida Eisenhower's quilts during the 1980s by The Textile Conservation Workshop, Inc., South

Salem, NY; Nancy Conlin Wyatt, Textile Conservation, Paris, TX; and
Marian Kamm, Registrar of the Dwight D. Eisenhower Presidential
Museum, Abilene, KS. At that time many of the quilts showed severe
deterioration and many were cleaned and covered with nylon tulle to
prevent further deterioration. Original repairs made by Ida were preserved. Conservation reports maintained by the museum record the
condition of the quilts prior to and after conservation procedures. The
quilts not on permanent display at the Eisenhower Center are stored
rolled in an environmentally controlled warehouse.

14. Duncan, 17.
15. Dwight D. Eisenhower, *At Ease, Stories I Tell to Friends* (Garden City,
    NY: Doubleday, 1967), 78. It is interesting to note that there is some
    confusion about where the wedding took place. Dwight D. Eisenhower
    stated in his book that his parents were married in the campus chapel
    by Rev. E. D. Slade; however, the September 24, 1885, *Lecompton Moni-
    tor* gives the following account:

    > MARRIED–At the residence of Rev. W. D. Stover, Wednesday even-
    > ing, September 23d, 1885, by Rev E. D. Slade, Mr. D. J. Eisenhower,
    > of Hope Kansas, and Miss Ida Stover of Lecompton, Kansas.
    >
    > About twenty of the friends and relatives were present to witness
    > the ceremony. A number of presents were bestowed by those in atten-
    > dance. We wish them a prosperous and happy voyage over the sea of
    > life, and may their bliss be unalloyed.

16. *Hope Herald,* 4 April 1885.
17. Milton D. Good's daughter was Rose Good Kretsinger (1886–1963).
    Rose Kretsinger received a degree in design from the Art Institute of
    Chicago in 1908, worked professionally as a jewelry designer, and trav-
    eled in Europe for a year. She began her quilting career at the age of
    forty after her mother died in an automobile accident. She found inspi-
    ration for her patterns in antique quilts, primarily appliques. Like many
    of her contemporaries, she hired professional quilters to execute her de-
    signs. Many of her quilts are now housed in the Spencer Museum on
    the University of Kansas in Lawrence. Although Ida Eisenhower and
    Rose Kretsinger lived much of their lives during the same time period
    and within about one hundred miles of each other, it is unlikely that
    either influenced the other's quilting. For further information, see Bar-
    bara Brackman, "Emporia, 1925–1950: Reflections on a Community"
    in *Kansas Quilts and Quilters* (Lawrence: University Press of Kansas,
    1993), 107–25.
18. Thomas Branigar, "No Villains–No Heroes, the David Eisenhower–
    Milton Good Controversy," *Kansas History* 15 (Autumn 1992), 168–79.
19. Jacob Eisenhower, David Eisenhower's father, built a house in Hope in

1884. See *Abilene Gazette*, 4 April 1884. Jacob also owned land in the business section of Hope, and to help David start his business, mortgaged the farm he planned to give David and used the money to build a store on the Main Street property. See Deed Book S, p. 628, Register of Deeds, Dickinson County Courthouse, Abilene, KS.
20. Branigar, 168–79.
21. Kenneth S. Davis, *Soldier of Democracy, A Biography of Dwight Eisenhower* (Garden City, NY: Doubleday, Doran, and Company, Inc., 1945), 34–38.
22. Duncan, 17.
23. Ibid., 11.
24. Davis, 41–43.
25. McCallum, 36.
26. The quilt said to have been made by Ida Eisenhower and now on display at the birthplace of Dwight D. Eisenhower is usually named Tumbling Block; however, there is a *Woman's Day* (ca. 1940) quilt pattern similar to the one Ida made called Jacob's Ladder. See Barbara Brackman, *Encyclopedia of Pieced Quilt Patterns* (Paducah, KY: American Quilter's Society, 1993), 26–27. The quilt displayed at the Eisenhower birthplace was made much earlier than the 1940s.
27. *Bryan-College Station Eagle*, 6 August 1989, 4c.
28. Eisenhower, 72.
29. Faber, 76.
30. Nona Brown Thompson, "Ida Stover Eisenhower, Mother of Six Distinguished Sons," *Kanhistique* 14 (February, 1989): 2.
31. Faber, 78.
32. Duncan, 25. Following is a quote from Ida Eisenhower, given in an interview in 1943: "I believe you're the only one that I've met since Dwight's become prominent who hasn't asked me why he's a fighter, chose to be, when I'm so against war. And since you haven't asked, I'm going to tell you. From childhood, I chose my way. He was free to choose his. War will never bring peace; but so long as there are those who make war, someone has to go to our defense."
33. Ibid., 10.

*Appendix A. Quilts made by Ida Stover Eisenhower stored at the
Dwight D. Eisenhower Museum in Abilene, Kansas.*

Each of these quilts was examined, photographed, and documented by the
authors during the summer of 1993. The quilts are listed in chronological
order and have the accession number assigned by the museum.

H-77   Wandering Foot (Turkey Tracks), ca. 1875, 83" by 68".
        Red and blue print cotton fabrics; white muslin cotton backing; backing
        turned to front as binding; hand pieced and hand quilted (8 to 9 stitches
        per inch).

H-1697 Six-Pointed Star with Hexagons, ca. 1875, 72" by 72".
        Green and white solid cotton fabrics; white muslin cotton backing;
        applied white binding; hand pieced and hand quilted (7 stitches per
        inch).

H-81   Nine Patch Variation, ca. 1875, 72" by 52".
        Red and brown cotton fabrics; red and black backing; backing turned to
        front as binding; hand pieced and hand quilted (8 to 9 stitches per inch).

H-78   Eight-Pointed Star (Evening Star), ca. 1875, 72" by 57".
        Red, brown, and black wool fabrics; wine striped cotton flannel backing;
        backing turned to front as binding; hand pieced and hand quilted (4
        stitches per inch).

H-1633 Four Patch and Sixteen Patch, ca. 1900, 72" by 62".
        Brown, tan, and gray cotton flannel fabrics; striped brown and white
        cotton backing; knife-edge binding; machine pieced and hand tied with
        yellow yarn.

H-80   Nine Patch Variation, ca. 1900, 66" by 59".
        Blue, tan, lavender, off-white cotton print and flannel fabrics; indigo-
        blue Nine Patch at center surrounded by plaid flannel Nine Patch
        blocks; lavender-and-white plaid flannel backing; backing turned to
        front as binding; hand pieced and hand tied with light green and aqua
        yarns.

H-75   Crazy Quilt containing Delegate Badge, ca. 1900, 80" by 72".
        Multicolored silk, cotton, velveteen, and velvet fabrics; cotton sateen
        backing; backing turned to front as binding; black velvet block initialed
        "I. E. E." (Ida Elizabeth Eisenhower) in gold colored thread; red ribbon
        with words "Delegate Badge, Department of Kansas, Salina, Jan'y 1890.
        9th Annual Encampment"; single patch rectangles and squares borders
        in varying widths; cotton sateen backing, backing turned to front as
        binding; machine pieced, decorative embroidery around patches
        stitched through to back.

H-74   Crazy Quilt, ca. 1900, 81" by 73".
        Multicolored silk, cotton, velveteen, and wool fabrics; four large crazy
        patch blocks with borders of one width on side and a different width

along the length; brown and gray striped cotton backing; black blind stitch as edging; decorative embroidery around patches; tied with orange and yellow yarns.

H-73   Crazy Quilt with Log Cabins and Fan, ca. 1900, 83" by 71". Multicolored cotton, wool, silk fabrics; borders of pieced rectangles on outside edge, center area contains recognizable shapes such as stars, hearts, log cabins, and fans; blue and white striped cotton flannel backing; backing turned to front as binding; decorative embroidery around patches stitched through to back.

H-82   Utility Quilt, ca. 1900, 83" by 66". Drab green, gray, brown, and tan heavy cotton and wool fabrics; blue-and-white cotton ticking backing; backing turned to front as binding varying in widths from 3/4" to 2"; machine pieced and tied with heavy white utility string.

H-1160 Single Patch Scrap Quilt, ca. 1900, 83" by 66". Multicolored silk, rayon, and cotton pillow ticking sewn in single rectangular and square patches; hand pieced and hand quilted (4 stitches per inch).

H-1597 Whole Cloth Comforter, ca. 1900, 86" by 68". Green and pink print cotton reversible fabric; tied with salmon pink yarn.

H-83   Velvet Crazy or Show Quilt, embroidered "1912", 64" by 42". Tan, purple, green, gold, red, pink, orange, and blue velvet fabrics; 25 full-circle, 15 half-circle, and 2 quarter-circle patches surrounded by border varying in width from 8" to 6"; chrysanthemum-flowered cotton print backing; cornflower-blue ribbon binding; elaborate embroidery around patches sewn through to backing.

H-79   Trip Around the World, ca. 1915, 85" by 64". Multicolored solid and print cotton and wool fabrics pieced in 3" squares; brown, gray, and white plaid cotton flannel backing; backing turned to front for binding; hand tied with red and orange yarn.

H-139   Trip Around the World, ca. 1915, 80" by 75". Multicolored cotton print and solid fabrics pieced in 3 1/2" squares with center of four red print squares surrounding one white square; two sides have applied bindings, other two sides have back turned to front for binding; machine and hand pieced; hand quilted (6 stitches per inch).

H-1191 Nine Patch in Two Sizes, ca. 1915, 90" by 74". Red, blue, tan, and white striped and gingham cotton fabrics; alternating rows of 9 1/2" square nine-patch blocks and 5" square nine-patch blocks joined with tan striped sashing; flour-sack backing imprinted with words "J E Brewer Abilene, Kansas"; machine pieced and hand quilted (6 stitches per inch).

H-1578 Old Maid's Puzzle and Twelve Patch, ca. 1915, 75" by 75". Blue, brown, red, and pink cotton print fabrics; alternating rows of twelve-patch blocks and Old Maid's Puzzle blocks set together with strips of red-and-white fabrics; white muslin backing containing imprints of bed springs; backing turned to front as binding; hand pieced and hand quilted (6 stitches per inch).

H-72   Grandmother's Flower Garden, ca. 1925, 79" by 69".
        Multicolored pastel print and white cotton fabrics; scalloped border with white applied binding; hand pieced and hand quilted (6 stitches per inch).

H-71   Nine Patch, ca. 1930, 84" by 59".
        Pastel print and solid cotton fabrics; Nine Patch blocks set together with white sashing and surrounded with yellow border; white muslin backing; white applied binding; hand pieced and hand quilted (5–7 stitches per inch).

H-76   Eight-Pointed Star, ca. 1930, 82" by 53".
        Pink, purple, yellow, and orange print and solid cotton fabrics; Star blocks set on diagonal with white cotton fabric surrounded with bright yellow border; white muslin backing; white binding; hand pieced and hand quilted (7 stitches per inch).

H-138   Eight-Pointed Star Top, ca. 1935, 86" by 66".
        Bright print and white cotton fabric Star blocks set on diagonal with white cotton fabric, surrounded by pieced yellow and white border with brown square set on diagonal; machine pieced.

H-137   Cherry Basket Top, ca. 1935, 98" by 81".
        Bright yellow print and white solid cotton fabrics; hand pieced with handles on baskets hand appliqued.

H-1156 Crazy Quilt Pillow, ca. 1900, 14" by 18".
        Multicolored cotton and wool fabrics; feather-stitch embroidery on crazy patches with seven Eisenhower boys' names embroidered on blocks; orange satin cord as binding.

H-1157 Crazy Quilt Pillow, ca. 1900, 18 1/2" by 18 1/2". Multicolored cotton and velvet fabrics; feather stitch embroidery on crazy patches with name "Ida" embroidered on top; orange satin cord binding.

H-1158 Crazy Quilt Pillow, ca. 1900, 17" by 19".
        Multicolored cotton and velvet fabrics; feather-stitch embroidery on crazy patches with name "David" embroidered on top; orange satin cord binding.

H-1159 Trip Around the World Pillow, ca. 1915, 18 1/2" by 17 3/4". Multicolored cotton print fabrics; postage-stamp-sized pieces arranged in Trip Around the World pattern;
        tan floral cotton backing; yellow cord binding.

H-1183 Irish Chain Pillow, ca. 1935, 16" by 16".
        Yellow and white solid cotton fabrics; white cotton backing, seamed edge around pillow.

The Quilt Designers
of North East England

Dorothy Osler

For a period from the late-nineteenth century to the mid-twentieth century, a quilting trade, apparently unique for its time, flourished in the North East of England. A small group of individuals, most trained by apprenticeship, set up business, drawing designs for quilting onto quilt tops. The quilt tops were either created by the designers, or produced by other quiltmakers of the region and then sent to the designers for quilting designs to be marked out. The majority of the tops were wholecloth ones but the designers also seamed "strippy" (Bars) and pieced tops to which quilting designs were added. They drew the designs by hand using a combination of outline pattern templates and freehand drawing. Customers added batting and backing to the tops, then quilted them. This paper describes how the trade operated, the quilts it produced, and the lifestyle and influence of one of the chief (and now most famous) practitioners, Elizabeth Sanderson.

For a period spanning the late-nineteenth century to the mid-twentieth century, a quilting trade, apparently unique for its time, flourished in the valleys of Weardale and Allendale, in the North Pennine Dales of North East England. A small group of individuals established a "cottage industry" working as quilt designers or quilt "stampers" (the colloquial term), marking out designs for quilting onto quilt tops.[1] The quilt tops were either created by the designers, or produced by other quiltmakers of the region, then sent to the designers for marking. The majority of the tops marked with quilting designs were wholecloth ones, but the designers also seamed "strippy" (Bars) and pieced tops to which quilting designs were added. The designs were drawn by hand with blue-coloured pencil using a combination of outline pattern templates and freehand drawing. The ready marked tops were commissioned or purchased by customers who added batting and backing to complete the quilts (which are referred to throughout this paper as "designed quilts").

The establishment of the quilt design trade has been attributed to a local draper, George Gardiner.[2] His shop in the village of Allenheads is thought to be where the trade began and where he trained apprentices. His known apprentices were all young girls or young women of whom Elizabeth Sanderson became the best-known and longest-established practitioner.

These quilt designers became very skilled and their style of pattern drafting shows a quality developed from training and practice. Their designs are elaborate but conform to identifiable lay-out plans and use a small but characteristic library of template patterns and fillers. Whether drawn on wholecloth, strippy, or pieced tops, the designs are stylistically unique and can therefore be traced and identified on quilts now dispersed around the world. (For a detailed description of this style, see the section on Characteristics below.)

Practitioners of the trade were apparently confined to the two dales of Allendale and Weardale, but customers came from a wider area, though still largely from North East England. Inexpensive and apparently well-known, the service was widely used both by individual quilters and by quilting groups because it provided a ready alternative for anyone unwilling to tackle that accepted difficulty in quiltmaking—marking out a quilting design of clarity and quality. Literally thousands of quilt tops were marked; hundreds still survive.

The quilts produced in this way from this region are rarely signed or dated but their special characteristics make them, for the most part, identifiable. The blue pencil marks are often still visible, the nature of the patterns and their disposition give a stylistically distinctive identification "mark," and the characteristic use of particular fabrics together with cotton batting are all hallmarks of these designed quilts. The purpose of this paper is to describe in detail how this trade operated, the characteristics of the quilts it produced, and the lifestyle and influence of one of the chief (and now most famous) designers, Elizabeth Sanderson.

The Place: Locality, Industry, and the Quiltmaking Tradition

Locality and Industry

Situated at the northerly end of the Pennine Hills in North East England, only a few miles of barren moorland divide Allendale and Weardale–the upper valleys of the Rivers Allen and Wear respectively (see figure 1). Though remote from metropolitan influence, these were not backward areas but had good communications, by road and later rail, with the urban centres of the region, in particular Newcastle upon Tyne.

For several hundred years prior to the twentieth century, the two dales had been economically important for the extraction of minerals, particularly lead. In the first part of the nineteenth century, the well-established lead-mining industry of the dales prospered in the wake of the Industrial Revolution. For much of the nineteenth century, a lively and relatively prosperous community, based on mineral extraction and hill farming, survived in the two dales. As lead mining expanded so too did the population; the 1861 census records 6,400 residents in Allendale, most of them born within the dale. Communities were therefore close–a network of interwoven family relationships (indicated by the commonality of certain surnames, including Sanderson) with shared experience and social activity. The consequent social and cultural practices were long-established and built upon the traditions of the district. Quiltmaking was just one such tradition; music-making was another.[3]

Prosperity did not, however, last. Like other rural areas of Britain, the dales suffered a level of rural depopulation from the mid-nineteenth century onwards as workers were drawn, or pushed, to the rapidly developing industrial areas of North East England, or even further afield. One celebrated incident of industrial strife in Allendale in 1849 led to sixty people emigrating to Galena, Illinois, where their lead-mining skills were presumably in demand.[4]

Towards the end of the nineteenth century, the lead-mining industry was hit by a severe slump because of a drop in the price of lead. It began in 1878 and reached a record low in 1892. The sudden collapse of mining activity led to mass migration from the dales as families left in search of work.

Quiltmaking in the Dales

Quiltmaking was already an established vernacular craft in the dales in the early nineteenth century though surviving quilts from this period are rare.[5] The dales tradition had developed from a wider British tradition of "country" quiltmaking which laid emphasis on the stitchery of quilting. While intricate patchwork and formal broderie perse appliqué became part of a genteel English lady's stitching repertoire, quilting wholecloth, strippy, and simpler patch-

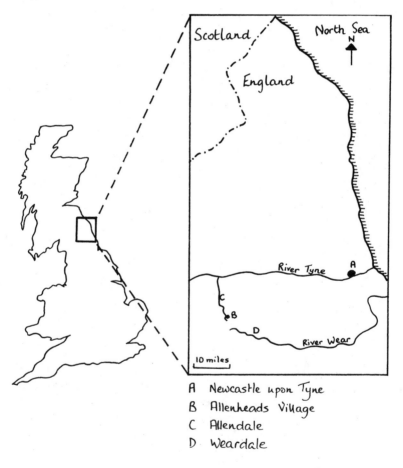

A   Newcastle upon Tyne
B   Allenheads Village
C   Allendale
D   Weardale

Figure 1. Location of Allendale and Weardale in North East England.

work and appliquéd quilts was common practice in certain rural parts of Britain in the eighteenth and nineteenth centuries, and part of rural folk lore.[6]

Quiltmaking remained a cultural practice throughout much of northern Britain in the nineteenth century, resulting in what are now referred to as "North Country quilts." An especially vibrant culture evolved in the North Pennine Dales. It produced some of the finest of nineteenth-century British quilts. Dales' quilters produced wholecloth and strippy quilts of confidence and quality but they also developed distinctive pieced and appliquéd designs. On these quilts the quilted designs reflect the long-established British pattern library of motifs and filler patterns used on both quilts and quilted clothing, but with added regionally distinctive patterns. For the most part, these regional patterns were stylized forms of leaves, flowers, and ferns but included sinuous chain and feather patterns. Perhaps it is in the nineteenth-century quilts of the dales that we see captured the confidence and creativity of these self-contained communities. Certainly, the range and quality of quilts rivals that from any other part of Britain.

Two aspects of nineteenth-century quiltmaking in the North Pennine Dales highlight the strength of the activity at that time. It is one of the few regions of Britain in which quilting "parties" were recorded where music, song, and dance mixed with quilting.[7] It is also one of the few regions of Britain which records quilts with an inward transatlantic influence; the red, white and green appliqué quilts produced in the second half of the nineteenth century appear to be copies of patterns circulating in America at that time.[8] It is perhaps a reflection of the dales quilters' confidence and ability that they were able to absorb and adapt to new ideas and influences. It was within this framework of an active quiltmaking culture with associated, high-quality, technical skills and design expertise that the quilt design trade developed.

The Quilt Design Trade: Initiation, Operation, and Evolution

Initial Beginning

Two particular questions surround the initiation of the quilt design trade: how, when, and why did it begin; and how did such a unique style apparently develop so quickly once trade commenced? Local archive and printed sources have proved essentially unrevealing. The designers appear not to have advertised nor kept any formal business accounts and, save for one business card, no personal papers (except paper template patterns) have come to light within the families of the now-deceased designers. It is from oral sources that information has been gathered; but such research has taken place almost entirely in the second half of the twentieth century—a generation too late to capture any *reliable* recollection of the early establishment of the trade and the gentleman who reputedly began it.[9]

The first written account of the quilt design trade was given by the late Mavis FitzRandolph in her classic book *Traditional Quilting*, and most subsequent accounts are based on this source.[10] Travelling the dales in the early 1950s with Florence Fletcher, a local quilter married to a mining engineer, FitzRandolph interviewed quilters, customers, and the surviving quilt designers. Her information came entirely from oral sources. She ascribed the establishment of the trade to a village shopkeeper, George Gardiner (1853–ca.1900):

> During the latter half of the nineteenth century a certain George Gardiner of Allendale, Northumberland, marked patterns on "quilt tops". . . . He kept the Allenheads village shop (and a lovely shop it was, as old people in the village will still tell you) in Mill Cottages, Dirt Pot. . . . He also trimmed hats, and girls would walk up from Allendale Town or over the fells from Wearhead and throughout Northumberland; he taught his wife's two nieces, who were brought up by the Gardiners, to quilt and mark patterns, and one of them is still active, but his most notable pupil was Elizabeth Sanderson, who served her time with him as an apprentice *and became even more famous than he.* [emphasis added][11]

What led a draper in a remote English village to do something only previously done (in a much earlier time period) for more sophisticated metropolitan markets—mark out quilting designs for paying customers?[12] FitzRandolph shed no light though she did comment: "He had many followers though I have been unable to discover whether he had any immediate predecessors to link him with the eighteenth-century markers."[13]

No known relatives of George Gardiner have survived, but census records reveal some biographical details.[14] He is first recorded in 1861 at the age of eight, listed as the grandson of Thomas and Elizabeth Sanderson of Cornfield Cottage, Allenheads. In 1871 (aged 18) he is recorded as living with his widowed grandmother (Elizabeth Sanderson, senior) in Allenheads, and described as a draper's shopman.[15] By 1881, George Gardiner was married to Sarah (a local girl, from a village two miles away) and described as a draper. He and his wife lived at Smelt Mill Cottages, Allenheads; they subsequently had no children. In 1891, George and Sarah Gardiner had apparently separated, with Sarah still living at Smelt Mill Cottages and described as a milliner (with the word "dress" added to the record in a clearly separate hand).[16] George is recorded still living in Allenheads as a boarder (lodger) in the home of a 59–year-old widow; he is still described as a draper. George Gardiner is said to have died before 1900 but the parish records contain no mention of his death.

Though the census records confirm he was a draper, no formal documentary evidence exists to confirm that George Gardiner did indeed begin the quilt design trade and no surviving quilts can be ascribed to his hand with certainty; however, there seems no reason to doubt the *main body* of information as recorded by Fitz-Randolph. The *Historical Directory, 1886* (a trade directory), however, does *not* record George Gardiner amongst the eleven "Grocers and Drapers" listed for Allenheads, though it does record a Mary Stephenson as a dressmaker at Mill Cottages.[17] This could suggest that George Gardiner did not have his own shop but worked for an employer.

As to when the quilt design trade began, FitzRandolph broadly suggested "the latter half of the nineteenth century."[18] It seems probable, though, that the quilt design trade followed on from the Gardiners' millinery trade which presumably developed following George's marriage to Sarah in 1876.[19] The likelihood is that quilt designing was added sometime in the 1880s.

Two factors may have had some influence on the establishment of the trade at that point in time. Firstly, the domestic sewing machine had become fairly commonplace in the previous 1870s decade and, as a draper, George Gardiner could have capitalized on its potential use in the traditional practice of quiltmaking, for which he presumably provided at least some supplies. Secondly, the 1880s

was a period of serious industrial decline in the dales. The dra-
matic slump in the fortunes of the lead-mining industry in the second half of the nineteenth century, when the price of lead collapsed,
and the consequent migration out of the dales badly affected those
businesses dependent on the community. This included shopkeepers of whom Gardiner was one.[20] Perhaps his divergence into quilt
designing was a response to the economic pressure of trying to sus-
tain a living amongst a declining community. If so, it appears to
have been successful.

If he began the quilt design trade, did he also set the style? George
Gardiner remains a mysterious figure with a lifestyle (indicated by
the census records) which did not accord with the norm for a man
of his background. Most men born into dales' families at that time
were apprenticed into one or other of the trades associated with
the lead-mining industry. Gardiner's grandfather, in whose family
he was raised, was an enginewright, as was one of his uncles in the
same household. Another uncle was a lead-ore miner. George, however, became a draper's shopman and eventually a draper. Did he
follow another line of business because it suited him better, either
for reasons of preference or physical capability?

Did he learn the millinery trade from his wife, Sarah, and develop a particular aptitude for it? Did they establish a textile business which combined dressmaking, millinery, and quilt designing
with general drapery? Was his new and innovative style of designing so admired that customers were only too eager to purchase
one of his designs for a "best" quilt. These questions are, and will
remain, conjecture, but the trade, once established, apparently prospered.

How the Trade Operated
The existence of the quilt designers during the period they were
active (ca.1880–ca.1960) appears to have been common knowledge
amongst women in North East England who either made quilts,
for whatever reason, or belonged to sewing groups, usually church
or chapel-based. (These sewing groups or clubs were a major social and fund-raising activity in communities throughout North East
England in the late-nineteenth and early-twentieth centuries.) Never
apparently advertised, the trade succeeded by word-of-mouth trans-
mission and recommendation. One designer in Weardale, Olive

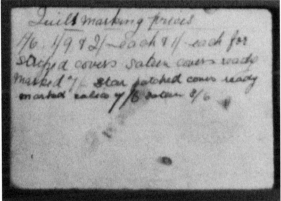

Figure 2. Olive Allinson's business card, front and back, with her prices for marking and for ready-marked tops. Weardale Museum.

Allinson, produced a business card, but she seems to have been a rare exception (see figure 2).[21]

Customers could avail themselves of the service in one of three ways: (1) they could order a ready marked quilt top, of specified type and colour, from a designer; (2) they could post a ready prepared (pieced or seamed) quilt top to a designer who would return the marked-out top by post; (3) they could purchase a ready marked quilt top from the stock of a travelling salesman.[22] The cost was low–the price for marking a wholecloth quilt design on customer-supplied fabric was £0.1s.6d (US$0.38) to £0.2s.0d ($0.50) depending on design.[23] Prices seem not to have varied greatly in the first half of the twentieth century, the period of activity best researched, though they did increase (to £0.5s.0d ($1.25)) in the 1950s. Olive Allinson's card (presumed to date from the 1930s) gives prices for purchasing a ready-marked top: "sateen covers [presumed wholecloth] 7/- [$1.75]; star patched covers ready marked, calico 7/6 [$1.88], sateen 8/6 [$2.15]." She also appears to have had a variable rate for marking out customers' tops "1/6 [$0.38], 1/9 [$0.44] & 2/- [$0.55] each & 1/- [$0.25] for striped covers."[24]

Once the trade was established, there must have been considerable customer demand for George Gardiner to establish the apprenticeship scheme which continued in an unbroken chain for the years of the trade's existence. Again, it was FitzRandolph who first recorded the details. She confirmed that Elizabeth Sanderson was one of Gardiner's apprentices (see above), then continued:

> [Elizabeth Sanderson] taught many girls to quilt and mark patterns [including] Mrs. Coulthard of Weardale [and] Mrs. [Jennie] Peart of Allendale [who] started work at the age of fourteen and served for a year without payment . . . she worked from eight in the morning till seven at night . . . and she served for six years being paid two shillings [$0.50] weekly in the second year and finally four shillings [$1]. In 1952 [Jennie Peart] was charging five shillings [$1.25] for marking out a quilt top . . . and has had one apprentice herself [Mary Fairless], who is still at work.[25]

This information must be regarded as accurate. It seems likely that FitzRandolph interviewed the two former apprentices mentioned, the late Jennie Peart (née Liddell) and Mary Fairless, who were both still living in Allendale in the 1950s. Mary Fairless lives there today (1997).

Customer Case Studies
From interviews conducted, mainly in the late 1970s and 1980s, I have selected the following case studies as representative of the overall research findings and to explain customer rationale in choosing to purchase a designed quilt. The case studies also highlight the type and condition of many of the surviving quilts.

• *Case Record 1.* Three wholecloth quilts were known to have been made by Louise Rutherford in Rothbury, Northumberland.[26] She married in the early years of the twentieth century but it was eight years before her first child was born. At a time when married women usually did not work unless family circumstances dictated otherwise, Mrs. Rutherford spent much of the early years of her marriage quilting. She sent to "someone in Allendale" (thirty miles away) for the quilt tops, all of which are cream-coloured cotton sateen with the blue pencil marks clearly visible. The quilts are all in near-perfect condition and had never been used or washed. Her daughter could give no technical information about how the quilts had been made.[27]

• *Case Record 2.* Four wholecloth quilts in the possession of a Northumberland lady had all been quilted by her maternal grandmother, a professional quilter. Like many women in North East coal-mining communities who needed additional income, she had established quilt "clubs," making quilts for customers who paid weekly in small instalments.[28] Most of the quilts produced in this way were either wholecloth or strippy quilts and their designs were simply crafted using a small library of North Country patterns.

Three of the quilts are typical of this genre but the fourth was a striking apple-green and cream sateen quilt, little used, and with all the hallmarks of a designed quilt—blue pencil marks, and the characteristic motifs and freehand patterns drawn in typical style. The owner explained that this quilt had been her own mother's wedding quilt and that her grandmother had sent to "someone in Allendale" for the quilt top, then quilted it herself as a wedding gift to her daughter (ca. 1920).[29]

It is significant that a professional quilter, well able to plan quilts herself, nevertheless called upon the services of a quilt designer to mark out a "special" quilt—in this case, her daughter's wedding quilt. It is an indication of the recognition accorded to the quality of the designers' work.

• *Case Record 3.* In 1988 I interviewed Mrs. Lister and Mrs. Ena Richardson, two neighbours in a mining village outside Consett, County Durham. One had four family quilts, the other seven. Amongst both small collections were three quilts which looked like designed quilts. Questioning the owners about their origins confirmed this initial identification. One quilt was a pink/yellow strippy quilt in cotton sateen, with a running feather pattern quilted down each strip (see figure 3). The owner identified this quilt as one which had been marked by Mrs. Gowland of Weardale, the only certain confirmation from an oral source that the designers marked strippy quilts.

The other two quilts—one a pink and white star quilt and the other a pink wholecloth, both in cotton sateen—were thought to have been produced by the village community quilting group in the 1920s. This group raised funds specifically for a village hall which was eventually opened in 1926. Groups of this kind (usually associated with churches and chapels) often quilted tops ordered from the Allendale/Weardale quilt designers. It was a cheap and simple option to the problem of producing an attractive and acceptable design from amongst a group of quilters of varying abilities whose chief interest was in stitching, not designing.

Characteristics of the North Pennine Dales' Designed Quilts

If the formal historical evidence for the quilt-design trade is sparse, then the many surviving quilts provide tangible evidence of a design style which appears to have been established, right from the time of George Gardiner's assumed introduction. Though it is rare to find designed quilts identical in every detail, close analysis has identified common features which can be used to describe and identify this particular stock of quilts. This section will describe the quilt-top types and the identifying characteristics of fabric type, colour palette, marked design, pattern disposition, and pattern library. Each of these has, in some way, features which are characteristic of these quilts.

Quilt-top Types
If surviving quilts do indeed represent contemporary popular choices, the four types of ready marked quilt tops produced by the designers were, in descending order of popularity:

- *Wholecloth quilts.* These were the main product, with three strips of 30" wide fabric machine-seamed together to produce a double-

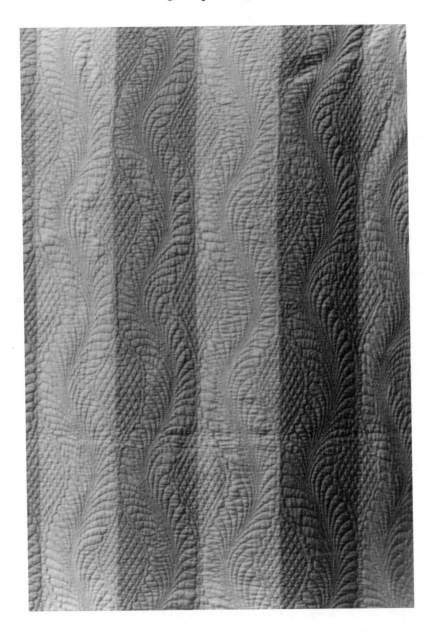

Figure 3. Strippy quilt in pink-and-yellow sateen marked with the running feather pattern by Mrs. Gowland of Weardale around 1920. Private collection.

bed-sized quilt top (see figure 4). Marked out in a day or less, these quilts were popular for eventual wedding gifts when completed by the customer.[30] Many survive because they were often "kept for best."

- *Star quilts.* The large, double eight-pointed star with five surrounding frames pieced in two colours was a bold design developed by Elizabeth Sanderson rather than George Gardiner (see figure 5).[31] Twenty-five of these Star quilts were brought to documen-

Figure 4. Wholecloth quilt in cream-coloured cotton sateen, late-nineteenth/early-twentieth century (97" x 108"). Courtesy of BEAMISH: North of England Open Air Museum.

tation days during the British Quilters' Guild three-year documentation programme.[32] Star quilt tops could be purchased or
commissioned from the quilt designers or bought from travelling salesmen.[33] Piecing and marking out the designs for these
tops was considered to be a job for the more skilled designers,
not inexperienced apprentices.[34] This star design, however, was
also copied by other quilters in the region.[35]

• *Pieced tops.* Pieced quilts with quilting designs that bear the characteristics of the quilt designers are known in collections. Most
have a direct and substantiated connection with Elizabeth Sanderson and include scrap mosaic patchworks, a Basket quilt, a Feath-
ered Star quilt, and a Streak o' Lightning quilt.[36] American design influence in these pieced tops cannot be discounted but the
popular North Country pink-and-white palette is also evident.
With the exception of the Basket quilt, now in the collection of
Beamish Museum, the tops were not pieced by Elizabeth Sanderson; she or one of the designers drew out the quilting patterns
either on the pieced tops or on the backing fabric.

• *Strippy tops.* Though strippy quilts were a popular North Country quilt type, only one survives that is known to be the product
of a quilt designer—a pink-and-yellow top marked by a Weardale
designer (see figure 3).[37] This absence of strippy quilts may reflect the fact that they were regarded as everyday quilts so even
"designed" strippies may have seen greater use and discard.
Equally, they were an easy type of quilt to piece and plan so
quilters may have felt more able to make their own strippy quilts
and therefore less need to purchase a top from a designer.

Quilt-top Fabrics

Cotton fabrics were most often used for all quilt types, with cotton
sateen for most wholecloth quilts. Cotton sateen was also popular
for star quilts, though a flat weave cotton was combined with Turkey red twill, as in the two star quilts still owned by Elizabeth
Sanderson's family.[38] Solid colours rather than prints were the norm.
Since the quilt designer only supplied the quilt top, the nature of
the wadding and backing was up to the customer to choose. In
practice, most quilts had a thickish cotton batting and were made
to be reversible, with a cotton or cotton sateen wholecloth backing
in the same or contrasting colour to the marked-out top.

Figure 5. Star quilt in turquoise-and-cream cotton sateen: ca. 1930 (82.5"
x 82.5"). Author's collection.

Colours

A small colour palette dominated, presumably as a result of customer choice and fabric availability. Cream-coloured sateen was
the most popular choice, followed by pastel shades of blue and
pink. Green and yellow were also popular in their varieties of apple
green and old-gold yellow (the darkest of the usual colour choices).
For star quilts, a two-colour combination was invariable with a
coloured fabric usually combined with white or ivory. So red/white,
yellow/white, green/white, pink/white, blue/white are the star quilt
colours, in the main, though some handsome exceptions, including an old-gold and brown star quilt, have been recorded.

Marked Designs

The quilt designers used blue pencil to mark out the design for the customer to quilt. The blue pencil lines are clearly visible on designed quilts unless they have been subjected to much use and laundering. A close look at the marked lines, especially on unquilted tops, is very revealing. Very evident is the skillful, confident pattern drafting that only comes from an experienced hand. Frequently, a particular pattern is repeated with slight variations, suggesting the addition of freehand elements to fill in from an outline template; sometimes the complete pattern appears to have been drawn freehand.

Disposition of the Designs

Most wholecloth quilts follow the typical layout of a central design, border, and filling pattern but each of those design fields has certain identifying features in the designed quilts from this region. First, the central design or central motif is large, often reaching out almost to the borders. It contains several motif patterns usually packed closely together and in an eight-fold arrangement (see figure 6). These motifs may be double- or triple-lined for clarity. The very centre of the design is usually a circular pattern. The whole central design flows outwards into the filling pattern, without formal containing lines. Within the design, pattern motifs or small areas between motifs may be filled with scrolls.

Second, border patterns connect at the corners with a motif or motif cluster, rather than turn the corner (see figure 7). Again, the border pattern flows inwards to the filling area, without the formal separating lines which could have been found on earlier quilting designs (see figure 8). Most borders include a degree of freehand pattern drawing as well as template pattern motifs (see illustrations). If a second border is present it is usually narrow, and not sharply separated from the main border.

Finally, the filling pattern itself is invariably square diamonds, usually drawn at no wider than 1" intervals and often closer. As would be expected of professional designers, these lines are accurate and correctly aligned (not always true of all North Country quilts).

Figure 6. Centre detail from off-white coloured wholecloth quilt in cotton sateen, showing one-quarter of the symmetrical centre pattern. Private collection.

Figure 7. Corner detail from an apple-green coloured wholecloth quilt in cotton sateen; corner patterns rarely flowed around corners but were interrupted by individual patterns or pattern groups. Private collection.

The Pattern Library

Two unique patterns which occur within the designed quilts can be regarded as trademarks. The first is the flat-iron, an oval shape in triple-lined form filled with a leaf or rose pattern, with added scrolls. The second trademark pattern, with no known ascribed name, is in the form of an open spiral with added plumed outline. It occurs in corners and centres but rarely in borders. In the absence of any signature, these trademark patterns can be positive identification marks for the designed quilts (see figure 9).

Other individual patterns, popular with the designers but not unique to them, include: the Lover's Knot, Sunflower, Feather Wreath, all circular patterns for the very centre of quilts; feather patterns, especially the large swirling Curved Feather; and large leaf and fern patterns together with variations of the circular rose— Single Rose and Double Rose, though not the Tudor Rose. Popular border patterns include the Swag (or Festoon), the Goosefeather, Fan and Half-bell with scrolls (figure 9). The use of freehand scrolls and scalloped, leafy-type patterns, both probably drawn freehand, to fill spaces between the pattern motifs is one of the most characteristic features of these designed quilts. They can be found in centres, corners and also in the space between the main border and quilt edge (see figures 4, 6, 7, and 8).

A word of caution, however. The above characteristics have to be considered together in order to surely identify a designed quilt. Most other North Country quilts were also made from cotton fabrics with cotton wadding, and the colour palette was similar. In imitation of the quilt designers, some were marked with blue pencil and used some of the characteristic patterns. It is the general combination, disposition and, most of all, the *quality* of the design which sets the designed quilts apart.

Origin and Influence of the Designers' Style

Before the middle of the nineteenth century, the quilt stitchery element on many traditional British quilts (as distinct from coverlets) was very pronounced, with elaborate designs quilted not only on wholecloth quilts but on medallion patchworks as well. These quilts usually had a commonality of quilting design. They used the central motif form set in well-defined borders with geometric divisions (arcs or zig-zag lines). The use of two parallel lines to define these

Figure 8. Classic border detail from a cream-coloured wholecloth quilt in cotton sateen. Private collection.

divisions was a central feature of most of these quilting designs and one retained by Welsh quilters right into the twentieth century. This gave a rigid, sculptured look to the quilts and cut off the borders from the central field of the design (see diagrammatic representation in figure 10).

This feature of defining lines is not present on the designed quilts, so allowing the pattern elements to flow together. Also, the designers used a pattern library with many more curvilinear patterns—rose, leaf, and feather patterns particularly. Together, these produced quilting designs with a fluid look. The size of the centres of the quilting designs also increased dramatically, creating large cen-

Figure 9. *(Opposite page)* Trademark and characteristic patterns from designed quilts: a. unnamed scroll and scallop pattern; b. triple-lined flat iron with rose, leaf, and scroll infill; c. swag border; d. goose-wing border; e. unnamed border. Patterns (a) and (b) can be considered trademark patterns since they are rarely found on other than designed quilts. Note the curvilinear nature of all the patterns and the combinations of scrolls and scallop outlines which, though similar in form, vary in detail.

tral features to hold the eye. But to the practical quilter, this also cut down the area to be filled with cross-hatching, a tedious and difficult task. Another apparent innovation on the designed quilts was the introduction of scattered, open scrolls and scalloped, leafy-type patterns, both of which were used as fillers in between other pattern motifs. The loose form of these scrolls is quite different from the formal tight spirals of Welsh quilts.

The fact that such marked, identifying features can be seen on the designed quilts would accord with a single, creative hand masterminding this change, as suggested by the oral evidence documented by FitzRandolph. Her evidence points to George Gardiner as the initial agent of change.

Once set, elements of this design style were transferred by other individual quilters in the North of England to their own quilts. Recognizing the qualities and practicalities inherent in the style of the designed quilts, quiltmakers sometimes copied the curvilinear pattern choice and fluid disposition of centres and borders, but they did not always have the same experience and skill. Such derivative quilts, like those produced by local church groups, often show a restricted pattern choice and an openness of design which looks amateurish when set alongside a quality designed quilt.

Elizabeth Sanderson (1861–1933)

The role of Elizabeth Sanderson in developing and extending the quilt design trade is more certain than that of her predecessor and possible mentor, George Gardiner. She is well remembered by surviving relatives, customers' families, dales' residents and, indeed, the families of her apprentices. Oral information has been obtained from all these sources.

Census details confirm that she was born Elizabeth Jane Sanderson in 1861, the eldest daughter of William and Mary Sanderson of Allenheads (at the head of Allendale). They further confirm her residence in Allenheads in 1871 and 1891 (though not in 1881, for whatever reason) and her death in 1933. Interestingly, none of the records available for consultation (i.e. up to 1891) record an *occupation* for her.[39] FitzRandolph confirmed, however, that she was taught the quilt design trade by George Gardiner, though at pre-

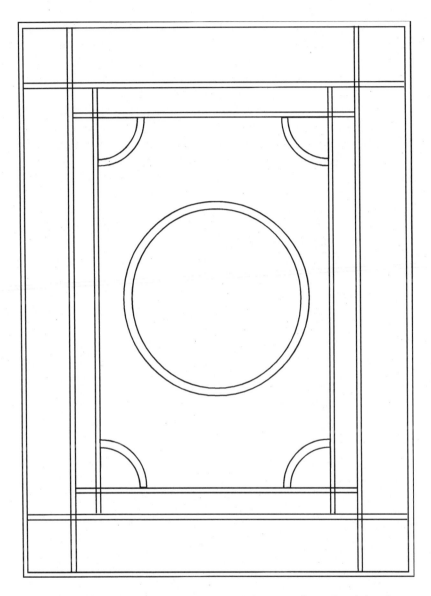

Figure 10. Diagrammatic representation of the central motif with borders and corners layout. The basic divisions of the quilt surface are formed by double rows of quilted lines, spaced 3/4"–1" apart, within which the pattern elements are arranged.

cisely what age she was apprenticed is uncertain.[40] Her apprenticeship must have post-dated the likely 1880s establishment of the
trade by George Gardiner (see above) but, since it is known she
took on her own first apprentice in the last decade of the nineteenth century, then a date around 1890 seems possible.

She spent all or most of her life living in the family home in
Allenheads until her death in December 1933 at the age of 72. By
that time she lived alone, but for much of her life her family unit
had included her sister, her brother, and her own son William,
born out of wedlock. Her sister kept house and her brother worked
locally, leaving Elizabeth free to supplement the household income
by quilt designing. Her output was prodigious; she is said to have
marked out quilt tops at the rate of one or two a day.[41] She never
appears to have advertised and no papers relating to her business
have survived, but the trade was so well known by word-of-mouth
that she seems never to have been short of work. Her niece, Bessie
Ripley, remembers the pile of cotton sateen waiting to be seamed
into quilt tops and the round mahogany table on which the fabric
was laid out for the designs to be drawn.[42]

Business was good enough for Elizabeth Sanderson to train her
own apprentices, beginning in the 1890s.[43] They began as young
girls, usually at fourteen years of age after leaving school, working
for a year as live-in apprentices without payment, then receiving a
small payment in the second year rising to £0.4s.0d [$1] per week
thereafter. Working hours (circa 1910) were from 8 o'clock in the
morning to 7 o'clock at night with a break for lunch and tea; Miss
Sanderson was reputedly a stern teacher with a "prim and exact-
ing" manner.[44] How many apprentices were trained is not known;
only some of those who went on to practice the trade in their
own right have been recorded. They include: Mrs. Coulthard of
Weardale, her first apprentice in the 1890s; Jennie Peart of Allendale, apprenticed around 1910 and who herself taught Mary Fairless
of Allendale; Olive Allinson (it is presumed), the sole designer
known to have produced a business card; and Frances Humble of
Weardale, known from mention in a letter to Shiela Betterton of
the American Museum in Bath (see figure 11). Shiela Betterton spent
some time in the North Pennine Dales in the 1970s and purchased
a marked star top from an elderly lady, Annie Dalton of Cowshill,
Weardale, who she met following a quilt sale.[45] This unquilted green-

Figure 11. Elizabeth Sanderson (far right) photographed around 1910 outside her home in Allenheads. With her are two apprentices; far left is Jennie Liddell, later Mrs. Peart. Courtesy of BEAMISH: North of England Open Air Museum.

and-white quilt top is now in the Heritage Collection of the Quilters Guild of Great Britain.

Although only a handful of surviving quilts can be ascribed to Sanderson's hand with certainty, their quality confirms her reputation as described by FitzRandolph. Many more surviving pieces are of such a quality, drawn with such sureness of hand and known to have been drawn out by "someone in Allendale" that they may well have come from her workroom. The bold, two-colour star design was indeed her invention (see note 31). Her pride in this design may be assumed from the fact that the two quilts left to her family, which she herself designed and quilted, are both star quilts.

Most of the quilts produced from the Allendale and Weardale designers, whilst rarely identical in every detail, do have a pattern set and disposition which marks them out as stock designs. In other words, once a successful product format was arrived at, it was followed with only the patterns varied slightly within the format for each quilt. The star quilts particularly show a uniformity of design; some of the wholecloth quilts from the 1920s have been documented with identical centre designs.[46] But although formats can be similar, the quality of draughtsmanship can vary. It is tempting to think that those of superior line quality, known to have come from Allendale and dating from the pre-World War II period were from Sanderson's workroom, but the lack of certainty is a frustration needing further research and analysis.

One set of quilts which has come to light in recent years does, however, bear witness to Elizabeth Sanderson's special talent. Three pieced quilts (two block designs and one Streak o' Lightning), known to have been made by village women in Allenheads and quilted communally, had their coarse, cotton backing material marked out for quilting by Sanderson.[47] The designs on these three quilts show an elaboration, experimentation, and quality of line that could only have come from someone with supreme skill and talent, allied to the experience and confidence gained in long practice. They were marked almost at the end of Elizabeth Sanderson's life but are of a style quite different to the designs that were her stock-in-trade. Marked out for neighbours and friends, they suggest a rare opportunity for experimentation.

Discussion

That the quilt design trade existed in Northern England and spanned the approximate period 1880–1960 is without doubt. Oral testimony, the surviving quilts, and the information recorded and published first by Mavis FitzRandolph, then others including Averil Colby and myself, all bear witness to the *fact* of the trade. The real questions are why such a unique operation began and how it came to produce quilts of such a quality and style—a style which seems to introduce new elements (a free-flowing form and "trademark" patterns) which differ from the regional style previously in use. So what were the factors that could have combined to allow this trade to develop in a corner of northern England?

From a cultural perspective, a vital factor was the prior existence of quiltmaking as part of regional culture in the North of England in the first half of the nineteenth century. Skilled quilters already existed to provide a pool of practitioners who recognized both the superior quality of design on the Allendale/Weardale quilts and the limitations of their own design skills. They were therefore willing, and able, to pay for a service which provided them with a ready marked quilt top to be turned into a handsome quilt. Only their stitching skills were required and then, as now, there was always pleasure in the making.

Because quiltmaking was an active vernacular craft in the region, and because the use of quilts as *top* bedcovers was common practice in most homes in North East England throughout the nineteenth century and early twentieth century, provision of such bedcovers provided a required domestic artifact. It was also a means of expressing a sense of belonging to that particular region of England with its attendant class and cultural overtones. So circumstances combined to provide a *market* for the trade product—a marked quilt top—which fitted with a domestic and cultural need and a widespread leisure and social practice.

From an economic perspective, the 1880s period, during which the trade apparently evolved, coincided with a period of serious industrial decline in the North Pennine Dales. Trade in Allenheads declined dramatically because of de-population so there was pressure on all traders, including Gardiner. Perhaps a need to diversify his trade base, combined, at that point in time, with the opportunity to provide quilt tops at relative speed (by seaming with the machine), "pushed" George Gardiner, an experienced draper with an apparent talent for millinery, into the establishment of the quilt-design trade. The paradox is that a trade and activity which became, quintessentially, a women's business and leisure occupation was begun by a man.

What of the style characteristics of the quilts themselves? The use of cotton sateen, cotton batting, and a largely pastel colour palette represents no more than was common practice in the quilt-making tradition of North East England as a whole over the historical period covered. The pattern disposition, too, with a central design set in a square-diamond field and bordered with one or, occasionally, more borders was the common design format for wholecloth quilts that had been in use in Britain for centuries. But within that format, these designed quilts did develop their own characteristics and unique pattern elements (see figure 9). That uniqueness seems to have been established at the outset, suggesting the influence of an individual creative hand. Since there seems no reason to dispute that George Gardiner began the quilt design trade, the assumption could be that it was his hand. It is certain, however, that Elizabeth Sanderson had a strong influence on subsequent design and since, where connections can be made, surviving quilts are linked to her rather than Gardiner, there is room for doubt as to which of the two had the greatest influence on the style of the designed quilts.

The research into this quilt design trade has highlighted aspects of English quiltmaking history that are worthy of comment. Despite extensive searches in an attempt to back up the known oral history of the trade, no newspaper articles, advertisements, letters, or documentary material of any kind came to light that gave any hint of the trade, save for the business card of Olive Allinson. Yet the existence of the trade is undeniable; so why should no formal mention be found?

One conclusion is that, save for George Gardiner, the practitioners and customers were women. It seems that the trade was given little formal status, either within the dales' community or within a wider social culture, by the men who usually recorded official documents. There are probably two reasons for this: first, it was an unusual trade, hard to "pigeon-hole" and therefore name; and secondly, it was a home-based textile trade and by the late-nineteenth century these had low status.[48] Even in census records, Elizabeth Sanderson, a woman known to have spent most of her life designing quilts, is given no occupational status.

If the trade was accorded little formal status during its lifetime, the quilts remain as evidence and testimony to a well-established cottage industry, and to a small group of skilled craftspeople whose development in time and place was a response to a unique combination of regional, cultural, economic and personality factors. The style and quality of these quilts will always speak in a way that few documents can for the individual quilt designers whose time, energy, skill and artistry went into their creation.

Acknowledgements

The author would like to thank the anonymous referees and the editor of *Uncoverings* for their very helpful comments which have greatly enhanced the focus of this paper.

Notes and References

1. This colloquial term may have arisen from the similarity of appearance between the blue pencil lines of the quilt designs to the blue stamped transfer lines of commercially available embroidery patterns. The term "designer" is unlikely to have been used within the communities of the dales or, indeed, throughout the North East region though it is a more appropriate designation for the activity.

2. Mavis FitzRandolph, *Traditional Quilting* (London: Batsford, 1954), 39–40.

3. Dorothy Osler, *Traditional British Quilts* (London: Batsford, 1987), 117.

4. Thomas Hutchinson, *Memories from Sinderhope* (unpublished, Northumberland Record Office, NRO 3469). Hutchinson records that sixty people left Allendale for Illinois on 17 May 1849, after an eighteen-week strike over hours and working conditions.

5. The diary of Thomas Dixon (1832–37), a lead-ore smelter of Dukesfield near Hexham in Northumberland, contains the following entry: "March 12 1832: Setting 'tatoes - very cold day with showers wind E - Jane twilting at our folks." The use of the colloquial term "twilting" for quilting is noteworthy; it was in common use in the region throughout the nineteenth century and later. (Diary information supplied by Dr Stafford Linsley, Department of Continuing Education, University of Newcastle upon Tyne).

6. Osler, 104–06.

7. Averil Colby, *Quilting* (London: Batsford, 1972), 142. Colby cited an entry entitled *Quilting Feast* from *A Glossary of the Dialect of Almondbury and Huddersfield* (Yorkshire) detailing quilting parties and the hospitality provided. More ironically, a footnote to the 1872 edition of Thomas Wilson's poem *The Pitman's Pay* (London: Routledge), originally published in 1843, reads as follows: "It was an awful sight for the male inmates of the house to see the quilting frame erected on the Monday morning, with many of the gossips in the vicinity set down to their highly important labour. The whole attention of the mistress was given to these lady stitchers, nothing else was properly attended to as long as this important labour continued. The best creature comforts were provided for them."

8. Osler, plates 5 and 6. It is likely that this transfer of design ideas was

brought about by returning émigrés, and by correspondence from emigrants who enclosed American newspaper and magazine articles in their letters to relatives in England.

9. Mavis FitzRandolph conducted research, in company with Florence Fletcher (then resident in Weardale) in the early 1950s. Tyne & Wear Museums established an Oral History Scheme in the late 1970s–tapes and transcripts are housed in the Shipley Art Gallery, Gateshead, Tyne & Wear. The Quilters Guild of Great Britain conducted a Tape Archive Programme in the early 1980s and a Quilt Documentation Programme between 1990–1993. I established an individual programme of oral research in the early 1980s before the publication of *Traditional British Quilts*. Insofar as the quilt designers are concerned, my information has come from three main sources: (1) relatives of practitioners i.e. those who worked as quilt designers either in Allendale or Weardale; (2) relatives of customers; or (3) residents or former residents of the two dales who remember the practice in operation but did not necessarily participate either as customers or practitioners.

10. FitzRandolph, 39–43. The information collected and recorded by Mavis FitzRandolph has formed the basis of most subsequent writing on this subject, including that of Averil Colby.

11. FitzRandolph, 39.

12. Ibid., 38–39. FitzRandolph cites the eighteenth-century Sussex schoolmaster, Walter Gale, who supplemented his income by drawing out quilting and embroidery designs.

13. Ibid., 39.

14. Northumberland Record Office, *Census of Population* (1851, 1861, 1871, 1881, 1891) and Registers of Births, Deaths and Marriages in the Parish of Allenheads. Population censuses in the UK are only available for general consultation in Public Record Offices after one hundred years have elapsed, so no census after 1891 could be consulted.

15. Sanderson was one of the common surnames in Allenheads in the nineteenth century. No apparent family connection existed between Elizabeth Sanderson, George Gardiner's grandmother, and Elizabeth Jane Sanderson, the quilt designer.

16. Northumberland Record Office, *Census of Population 1891*.

17. *Historical Directory, 1886*, consulted in Newcastle City Reference Library. Interestingly, the 1881 census record includes Mary Stephenson and her cousin Mary Scott as living with the Gardiners at Smelt Mill Cottage and describes them both as dressmakers. Were these the "wife's cousins" referred to by Mavis FitzRandolph?

18. FitzRandolph, 39.

19. Northumberland Record Office, Marriage Register, Church of St Peter, Allenheads. The register recorded the marriage of George Gardiner, 23, draper to Sarah Stokoe, 23(4), spinster. No occupation was recorded for

Sarah at the time of her marriage but she was described in the 1881 Census as a milliner.

20. H. Dixon, *An Allendale Miscellany* (Newcastle: Frank Graham, 1974), 74. Dixon commented on the late nineteenth-century depopulation in Allendale: "The effects of depopulation were probably felt most acutely by local retailers or shopkeepers. Allenheads had fourteen of them . . . now there are fewer than six in the whole area [Allendale]."

21. Collections of the Weardale Museum, St John's Chapel, County Durham.

22. More than seventy travelling salesmen operated in Northumberland, mostly based in Newcastle upon Tyne, in 1894 (*Kelly's Directory of Northumberland, 1894*). The North East region had a good train network by that time and horse-drawn transport operated regularly between villages, towns, and railway stations.

23. In 1910 the exchange rate was US$4.868/£1; all conversions have been worked on an approximate basis of $5/£1. For a price comparison to these quilt-marking charges, in 1910 the average wage of an agricultural worker was £1.15s.4d ($8.84) per week. In 1911, the average annual miner's wage was £84 ($420) per year. Data on exchange rates and wages are from B. R. Mitchell, *British Historical Statistics* (Cambridge: Cambridge University Press, 1988).

24. Olive Allinson's business card has these hand-written prices on the reverse. The date of the card is unknown.

25. FitzRandolph, 40–43.

26. The quilts were originally owned by the quiltmaker's daughter. Two are now in the author's collection.

27. Mrs. Ramshaw, Louise Rutherford's daughter, Newcastle upon Tyne, interviewed by author, October 1985.

28. Osler, 122–25.

29. Mrs. Scales of Hepscott, Northumberland, interviewed by author, June 1984. Mrs. Scales' grandmother lived in the mining village of Murton, County Durham, in the early 1900s.

30. Mrs. Bessie Ripley, Stanhope, County Durham, Elizabeth Sanderson's niece, interview by author, May 1985.

31. The theory that the star design was developed by Elizabeth Sanderson was confirmed to me in an interview with her granddaughter-in-law, Mrs. Monica Sanderson, Allendale, April 1997.

32. *Quilt Treasures: The Quilters' Guild Heritage Search* (London: Deirdre McDonald, 1995), 108.

33. FitzRandolph, 40.

34. Mrs. Bessie Ripley.

35. One pink-and-white star quilt, of unknown origin, in my collection I believe to be a copy. With a slightly smaller central star and simpler quilt-

ing designs, its quality is not quite to the standard of the "designed" star quilts.

36. Rosemary E. Allan, *North Country Quilts and Coverlets* (Stanley, Co. Durham: Beamish Museum, 1987), 68. Other examples are in private collections.

37. Collection of Mrs. Lister, Castleside, near Consett, County Durham, photographed in 1988.

38. Two surviving grandsons of Elizabeth Sanderson, the sons of her son William, each have a Turkey red-and-white star quilt.

39. Northumberland Record Office, *Census of Population* (1871, 1881, 1891).

40. FitzRandolph, 39.

41. Mrs. Bessie Ripley. See also FitzRandolph, 40.

42. Bessie Ripley gave no clue as to size of the marking table but it was possibly one of the round dining tables on a central pedestal, common at the time and around five feet in diameter. It would probably not have accommodated the full quilt top.

43. FitzRandolph, 40.

44. Mrs. Bessie Ripley. Working from the known facts—i.e. charges for marking, known production rate, apprentices' pay and conditions—it is possible to hypothesize a potential profit margin for Elizabeth Sanderson's workshop around 1910. Assume that she marked out seven tops per week, on average, and that for five of these she supplied the material (9 yards of sateen). Profit for marking would have been £0.1s.6d ($0.38) x 7 = £0.10s.6d ($2.66) per week; if fabric was purchased wholesale with a 100 percent mark-up, then profit could have been approximately £0.10s ($2.50) per week. This assumes a wholesale cost of 3d ($0.06) per yard of sateen. Total profit = approximately £1 ($5), less payment to apprentices (1 @ £0.4s ($1) per week, another working for no payment) and the cost of weekly boarding for apprentices. Working on these loose assumptions, Elizabeth Sanderson could have been earning about half the average man's weekly wage of the period.

45. Correspondence between Shiela Betterton and Annie Dalton in author's collection. The correspondence includes the following extract in a letter, dated "Sept 10th 1971," to Shiela Betterton from Mrs. Dalton: "they were all drawn out by Frances Humble who walked over the fells to be taught by Miss Sanderson Allenheads. I quilted one for a granchild [sic] which had been left all run together [seamed] and traced ready. Now at the sale I bought a top all stitched together in the star pattern like my blue & white & already traced . . . It is in green & white, it is not thick cotton but the colours will be fast colours, as I will never do it now."

46. Two quilts documented during the Quilters' Guild Documentation Pro-

ject at the documentation day at the Bowes Museum, Barnard Castle, County Durham, had identical centre designs.
47. Mrs. Wright, Allenheads, interview by author, September 1995.
48. D. J. Rowe, "Occupations in Northumberland and Co. Durham, 1851–1911," *Northern History* 8 (1973). Rowe does not cite *any* textile occupations; it is presumed they come under his "twenty per cent of occupations not covered by the statistics" (p. 123). He does, however, cite female non-activity rates from 1851 to 1911 for the County of Northumberland, which includes Allendale. These drop only slightly from 80 percent in 1851 to 77.2 percent in 1911 (table, Occupations).

Mary Susan Rice
and the Missionary Quilt

Tracy W. Barron

An album quilt made in 1847 for Mary Susan Rice by the Female Missionary Sewing Circle of Lincoln, Massachusetts, reveals a story as involved as the quilt's construction. Beyond the remarkable fact that the quilt traveled to Persia and back, the quilt has an interesting history. Using unpublished journals, letters, and town records the author shows how a seemingly straight-forward album quilt has a complex contextual design. A detailed analysis of the inscriptions and their relative positions on the quilt revealed facts about the owner, the donors, a pioneering educator, an unusual educational institution, and certain nineteenth-century religious beliefs. Analysis of Rice's album quilt also revealed characteristics it has in common with other album quilts made in New England in the fourth and fifth decades of the nineteenth century.

On June 27, 1847, twenty-six-year-old Mary Susan Rice sat in her cabin on board the barque Catalpa, writing in her journal. She noted that the Catalpa "originally built for a packet between Boston and Charleston S.C. . . . [being] about 100 feet long and 24 1/2 feet wide" was already six hundred miles east of Boston, Massachusetts, en route to Asia where Rice was to start her work as a missionary to the Nestorians.[1] Mary Susan Rice's feelings were low as she "remembered the quiet Sab[bath] mornings in [her] own dear home . . . [and] fancied [her]self moving about the lower rooms or stopping to gase [sic] from the south windows upon the landscape that spread itself . . . in unsurpassed loveliness."[2] The home for which

Mary Susan Rice longed was in Lincoln, Massachusetts, a bucolic farm town seventeen miles west of Boston where she had lived with her parents and eight brothers and sisters (see figure 1). In the middle of a seemingly endless rolling ocean, this young woman yearned for the familiarity of the Hunt-Rice Tavern with its murals of exotic trees and stable mountain ranges (see figure 2).

Mary Susan Rice

Born in 1821, Mary Susan Rice was, if the photograph taken of her later in life is reliable, a not unattractive young woman when she left the United States for Persia (see figure 3). That she was an intelligent woman and a devout Christian is indisputable. Her intelligence was nurtured in the Lincoln public schools in which the precedent for a liberal education for women was already firmly established.[3] In 1837, Elizabeth Farrar, wife of another Lincoln native, wrote in her well-known book, *The Young Lady's Friend*, "if you have regarded your studies as daily tasks to be performed till a certain period, when you will be released from them, you are still *uneducated* . . . and your intellectual powers . . . will dwindle away."[4] It is possible that Mary Susan Rice may have read Farrar's book;

Figure 1: The Hunt-Rice Tavern, Mary Susan Rice's home, in Lincoln, Massachusetts. Photograph by author.

Figure 2: One of the murals on the walls of the Rice home. It is attributed to the nineteenth-century itinerant artist, Rufus Porter. Photograph
by author.

she certainly continued her own education. Rice taught school in
neighboring towns before she entered Mount Holyoke Female Seminary in 1846 as a "senior student."[5] This school, founded by Mary
Lyon, gave "a practical domestic education, with intellectual instruction to a large number of female students."[6] Mount Holyoke,
however, was no mere finishing school; the school's curriculum
included Euclid, botany, mental philosophy, Latin, and Alexander's
Evidences of Christianity.[7] Rice continued to show an inquiring
mind, expressing her interest in learning navigation from the cap-
tain of the Catalpa (3 July 1847) and later in learning to speak and
read Syriac, the ancient Nestorian form of Aramaic.[8]

Rice's Christian faith was sincere and unwavering. She was leaving everyone whom she knew and loved to go to an unknown country as a missionary. Later in the voyage she wrote that as the ship
sailed "onward by each favoring gale to my adopted home, . . .
dearly [as I] love my New England home and still more dearly the
friends who make that home, a pleasant one, yet when Jesus calls,
I may gladly hasten to lands where darkness dwells, where sin

Figure 3: Privately owned
photograph of Mary Susan
Rice, taken around 1895.

abounds and the imploring hands of millions are waiting to receive
the bread of life."[9]

Together with two missionary couples, Mary Susan Rice was to
remain on board the Catalpa for two months before disembarking.
Rice's eventual destination was an American mission in Oroomiah,
Persia (now Rezaiyeh, Iran) where she would teach at the Fiske
Girls' School (see figure 4).[10] As the voyage lengthened, she still
thought wistfully of her home town. Once after being becalmed
for several days, the renewed movement of the ship made Rice
dream of her Massachusetts home:

> The wind has changed and we are moving on our true course once
> more. Last night I went to Lincoln in my dreams and was with Mary
> G. Her brother brought out a beautiful young horse of a sorrel color
> . . . for me to ride. He darted off like the wind, now rearing, now plung-
> ing. Still I retained my seat while friends looked on with some con-
> cern.[11]

The motion of the waves probably prompted Rice to dream of
the motion of a horse ride. The retention of her "saddle" and the
"concern" of her "friends" is also a meaningful component of
the dream. Keeping her saddle may reflect this woman's determi-
nation to succeed in her venture. The concern of her friends was

understandable. The mortality rate for missionaries, particularly women, was high and well known.[12] Letters giving vital news to and from missionaries took several months in transit; a sick missionary could die long before her family even knew she had been ill.

In order to remember her family and friends and acquaintances, many of whom she might never see again, Mary Susan Rice had packed an album quilt in one of her trunks. Perhaps she was referring to the still-packed quilt when on 31 July 1847, she wrote in her journal, "I am looking forward to the day when some fresh token of remembrance shall remind me of the loved and loving ones I have left behind."[13]

Made for Rice by the Lincoln Ladies' Missionary Sewing Circle, this quilt is still owned by Mary Susan Rice's descendants. I shall refer to it as the missionary quilt (see figure 5).[14]

Figure 4: Female School in Oroomiah, Persia. Illustration taken from *Woman and Her Savior in Persia* by A Returned Missionary [Thomas Laurie] (Boston: Gould and Lincoln, 1863), 37.

Purpose

An examination and analysis of the missionary quilt reveals messages that Mary Susan Rice took with her to Persia, messages that are pertinent both to her and to those whom she was leaving. The position of the various blocks seems quite deliberate and important to the quilt's overall meaning. A great deal of thought must have gone into the quilt top's arrangement. The Sewing Circle members who contributed to this album quilt meant for it to be not only a symbol of their affection and support but also a testament to read over and over as Mary Susan Rice pursued her missionary vocation. Both its form and content can be read a century and a half later as a way of understanding the hopes, fears, and beliefs of these nineteenth-century women. Rice's quilt also illustrates certain regional characteristics that it shares with other New England album quilts made between 1840 and 1860.

Lincoln Female Missionary Sewing Circle

The Lincoln Female Missionary Sewing Circle, an organization in which Mary Susan Rice was an active member, was formed by members of the First Parish Congregational Church.[15] Its stated purpose was "to render aid in the great enterprise of Foreign and Home Missions."[16] In order to accomplish this lofty goal, the members met once a month and sewed items that they would eventually sell at a special fair held every December. During these all-day monthly gatherings, members would socialize and listen to "missionary intelligence" (ie., letters, tracts, books on the subject of foreign missions) while they knitted and sewed, making fancy work, linen work, and patchwork. The Sewing Circle was a very popular organization; at one meeting the minutes note that there were "about one hundred present."[17] From its founding in 1842 until 1863, when the Soldiers' Aid Society claimed the attention and emotions of Lincoln's female population, the Female Missionary Sewing Circle seems to have been the primary philanthropic outlet for women in Lincoln, Massachusetts. Though its focus changed over the years, the Sewing Circle remained in existence until 1926.

Figure 5: Mary Susan Rice's missionary quilt is privately owned by one of her descendants who lives in Lincoln, Massachusetts. It is so large that the cut-out corners have been folded up at the end of the bed. Photograph by author.

One can imagine the excitement, even the awe, the Sewing Circle must have felt when in June 1846 Rice announced that she was going to be a missionary. A portion of the money the Sewing Circle sent to the American Board of Commissioners of Foreign Missions (ABCFM) would be going to support one of its own members. The circle immediately began to help Rice in her preparations. It also started an album quilt that she could take with her on her journey to the Near East.

Quilts of the Female Missionary Sewing Circle

The Sewing Circle's minutes show that Mary Susan Rice had been present when other album quilts were made. She was the secretary of the Sewing Circle at the July meeting in 1843 when she recorded that, "The Album Bedquilt was alluded to and the ladies were requested to bring their squares to the next meeting."[18] This entry also confirms the procedure of each member making her own square. This particular quilt was covered with Biblical quotations; Rice noted in September 1843 that "Several squares of the Missionary Bedquilt were brought in and the verses were read from them instead of a portion from the Scripture."[19] Another entry noting "the ladies being engaged in quilting the Album bedquilt" indicates that the actual quilting was a group effort.[20]

In June 1846 the minutes state that, "It was thought advisable to appoint an extra meeting for the purpose of getting the quilt in readiness for quilting as Mrs. Farrar offered to have it done at her house."[21] By August of that year, this particular quilt was finished and was evidently so admired by the same Mrs. Farrar that she purchased it then rather than wait for the annual December Fair.[22] Prior to 1847, the sewing circle seemed to make album quilts only to raise money for its mission work.

After Mrs. Farrar's quilt, the next quilt that the Sewing Circle made was for Mary Susan Rice; it was the first album quilt the Lincoln Sewing Circle made for a specific person. The minutes of March 1847 state: "The intention of rendering our assistance to Miss S. Rice was again brought up and heartily responded to by all present. The ladies decided that an album bed quilt should be made, each member making a square."[23] Rice would be leaving for Persia in June 1847, so the Sewing Circle had only a little over two months to make the quilt.

Description of Rice's Missionary Album Quilt

Mary Susan Rice's missionary quilt is 109 inches wide by 96 inches long and has two cut-out corners. The cut corners form a kind of T-shape which, according to Jeannette Lasansky, is "a New England phenomenon" (see figure 6). [24] The quilt's large size is probably due to Mary Susan Rice's numerous friends and acquaintances, all of whom wanted to contribute to its construction and its penned sentiments. It is a true scrap quilt in that there is a huge variety of materials making up its eighty-two squares (see figure 5).

Rice's quilt does not have one organizing pieced pattern. Though most of the squares are a simple Nine Patch, there are also nine squares in the Cross Ties pattern, one Pinwheel square, and one in the Anvil pattern. The organizational integrity of this quilt seems to come from the eighty-two white squares in the center of each pieced block and from the vivid yellow vertical sashing. When seen from a distance, the missionary quilt appears to be a strippy quilt. The horizontal brown sashing is less obvious since the brown fabric is quite similar to many of muted colors used in the various pieced blocks. In constructing the quilt top, a short horizontal piece of brown sashing was sewn to the top or bottom of each member's contribution. When a vertical strip of seven or nine joined squares was completed, it was sewn to another strip of blocks separated by the vertical yellow sashing.

The quilt back is a tan printed cotton and the binding is the same yellow fabric used in the vertical sashing. The quilt is not heavily quilted; the quilting follows each block's piecing. The light quilting confirms Linda Lipsett's observation that friendship quilts were lightly quilted because they were made for their sentimental value and not for hard everyday use.[25] The varied colors on Rice's quilt are still quite strong, indicating that it may not have seen heavy use or harsh washings.

Figure 6: Part of the quilt showing its cut-corners. Photograph by author.

The inscriptions in the missionary quilt's centered white squares range from simple signatures and formulaic sentiments like "Remember me," to biblical verses from the Old and New Testaments; there are also personal messages and original poetry. Only seven of the eighty-two inscriptions written in the central white squares are illegible; of those that are legible, sixty-eight are signed by different people. The format of Rice's quilt confirms Jacqueline Atkins's statement in *Shared Threads* that the "Inscriptions in both album books and quilts followed similar formats, all executed in the best Victorian calligraphy—a sentimental verse or biblical passage, the signature of the well wisher [and] a date."[26]

New England Album Quilts of the 1840s and 1850s

Like other album quilts that were made during the nineteenth century, Rice's quilt was "a gift from those closest to her [that would] commemorate this significant event in her life and serve as a reminder of her place among the group that cared for and supported her."[27] Linda Lipsett has noted that "friendship quilts made within a certain area, within the same period, often share many of the same characteristics, including pattern blocks, sashings between blocks, [and] . . . similar quilting patterns."[28] Rice's quilt has certain characteristics that are common to other album quilts made in New England in the 1840s and 1850s.

One of these regional characteristics is an over-all set of simply pieced squares.[29] The blocks' fabrics were usually an eclectic array of muted colors with no particular unifying color. During this twenty year period, the organizing factor in most of these quilts was the use of uninterrupted horizontal, vertical, or diagonal narrow sashings. The sashing was usually in a color not used in any of the pieced blocks and it almost always constituted the dominant overall motif. New England album quilts in this time period are also similar in the absence of wide, framing borders. In my survey of New England album quilts in this twenty year period, I found none with any applique work.[30] Made to commemorate the birth of a child, a small Massachusetts album quilt top contains all of these characteristics (see Figure 7).[31]

Most of the New England quilts I studied were all made for

Figure 7: An 1840s Massachusetts album quilt top illustrating character-istics common to many New England album quilts made between 1840 and 1860. Property of Vivien Sayre of Acton, Massachusetts. Photograph by author.

women who were staying in North America; most of them were moving west. Ricky Clark noted, "it is hardly coincidental that signature quilts were most popular during the period of America's westward expansion."[32] Mary Susan Rice's quilt, however, commemorates a most unusual event—the departure of a single woman to the "heathen" lands of the Near East.

Rice's quilt has a carefully planned textual construction; many of the messages penned on each square's center relate to those in adjoining blocks. Rice had been involved in making other album quilts with the Sewing Circle. Since she was still an active member of the Missionary Sewing Circle, she probably played a part in organizing the various squares that went in her own quilt.

The squares were not randomly sewn together but placed according to the significance of the text or the contributor; many are related in imagery or idea to contiguous squares.[33] Since the quilt top was constructed in vertical strips, the textual relationships can be read vertically and, in some cases, horizontally as well. Many of the New England album quilts in my research were set diagonally on point. I believe the Sewing Circle decided on a rectilinear set in order to facilitate the juxtaposition of the various inscribed messages. Though there were only a few monthly meetings when the Sewing Circle would be able to work on the quilt, it was still carefully planned.

In order to decipher the text of Rice's quilt, I assigned the vertical columns letters A through I and the horizontal rows numbers from one through ten (see figure 8). An examination of the careful placement of the various pieced squares will reveal what the ladies of the Lincoln Missionary Sewing Circle and Rice, herself, might have wanted to be highlighted when she used the quilt in Persia. The appendix lists all of the quilt's messages.

The Family Blessing

The squares placed in the exact center of Rice's quilt are organized into meaningful messages that she would always have before her when she looked at her quilt. The most important of these messages lie in rows 5 and 6, which together form the midline on the bed. Within these two rows is the focal point of the entire quilt. The central blocks E-5 and E-6 each have four blocks above, below, and on each side (see the darkest squares in figure 7). In this position they seem very important in the overall textual design.

E-5 is signed by James Rice, Mary Susan Rice's younger brother. This is the only block signed by a man and the only block that repeats the text written on another block. Both block E-5 and B-5 state Jesus' directive to his followers as written in Mark: "Go ye into all the world and preach the gospel to every creature." The repetition of this biblical passage emphasizes the importance of Jesus' call to mission. The inclusion of a man's signature under this direct call to mission work, in effect, legitimized Mary Susan Rice's vocation. Mary Lyon, the founder of Mount Holyoke Female Seminary which Rice had attended in 1846, had been unequivocal about a woman's having the approval of a family member in order to become a missionary: "young ladies must not only be willing to go, but must also have the approbation of father, mother, or perhaps brother or sister or sister's husband."[34] The emphasis in Lyon's

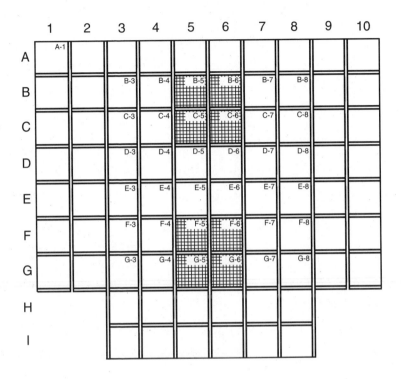

Figure 8: Diagram of missionary quilt that Mary Susan Rice took to
Persia in 1847. Drafted by Persis Barron.

directive is on male approval; in 1847 women were totally reliant
on masculine sufferance. The inclusion of James Rice on square E-
5 certainly addresses the issue of masculine "approbation."

The absence of Mary Susan Rice's father's name from the quilt
is, I believe, more significant than if it had been included along
with the other family members. Mary Susan Rice would never have
been able to go to Mount Holyoke without Henry Rice's blessing
and financial support. She certainly would not have been able to
go to Persia without Henry Rice's consent. Given his daughter's
religious convictions which he probably also espoused, Henry Rice
must have given his reluctant approval.[35] Stories of "martyr[ed missionary women] in the early expeditions were well known and often retold . . . throughout New England."[36] Signing a quilt square
may have been more than he could bear–almost like signing his
daughter's life away.

Mary Rice, Mary Susan Rice's mother, did sign the quilt . Square E-6 is next to the brother's blessing and is the most touching sentiment on the entire quilt. Mary Rice's distress at parting with her first born child is evident:

> Father to thee
> I yield the trust. O bless her with a love
> Deeper and purer, stronger far than mine.
> Shield her from sin, from sorrow and from pain.
> But should thy wisdom deem affliction best,
> Let love be mingled with the chastening.
> With an unshrinking heart I give her, Lord, to thee.
> Thy will not mine be done.

It is not difficult to infer from this inscription that Mary Rice never expected to see her beloved daughter again. In every monthly meeting of the Missionary Sewing Circle, news of the triumphs and tragedies of mission work was disseminated; everyone knew of women who had died in some distant mission station.[37] Many of those from Mount Holyoke who went with their husbands had been such casualties. Emma Bliss died in Persia in 1838, three months after arriving, and Prudence Richardson Walker died in West Africa in 1841, three months after she arrived.[38] These were just two of the deaths incurred in God's service. The Sewing Circle expected Rice to be one of the martyrs; the minutes state, "until recently we . . . little expected she would be permitted to speak to us again."[39]

If Mary Susan Rice did not die of some disease, the dangers she would encounter just in getting to Persia were well-known. Rice confirmed some of the dangers, writing in her diary of looking out and seeing "a large vessel only a few feet from my window, bearing directly down upon us."[40] Later she wrote that "we were pursued by a schooner suspected to be a privateer or pirate for two days."[41] If Mary Rice had these dangers in mind, her prayer on E-6 is a testament to her faith in God and her acceptance of the probability of the loss of her oldest child.

Blocks D-5 and D-6 are connected both literally and figuratively to the two central squares. Caroline Rice's signature is above her brother's on block D-5; she chose a hopeful passage from Psalm 121 concerning God's protection during the night (when, presumably, Rice would be using the quilt). The blessing on block D-6 was signed by Susanna Sherburne, Mary Susan Rice's aunt and namesake. The four blocks by Mary Susan Rice's brother, mother, sister, and aunt form a unit–a textual central medallion (figure 9).

In column 7, next to the maternal sentiment on E-6 and the aunt's on D-6, two other sisters' squares have been aligned with and form a part of the central medallion. On E-7 is Louisa Rice's optimistic choice from Revelations that also has a nighttime theme. Directly above on D-7 is Catherine Rice's scriptural quotation from Isaiah 27 counseling trust in God's strength. The grouping of the blocks of six family members would remind Mary Susan Rice continually of her family's support and prayers.

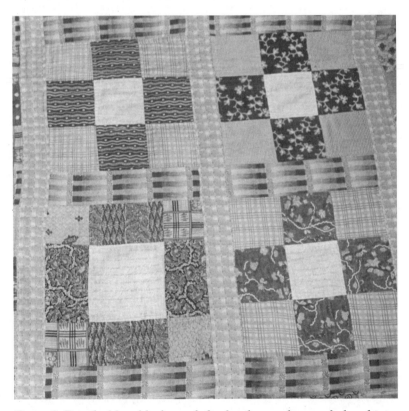

Figure 9: Detail of four blocks made by family members and placed in the exact center of Mary Susan Rice's quilt. The large white square was signed by Mary Susan Rice's mother; the two other blocks on the right are two more Rice sisters. Photograph by author.

Friends' Blessings in the Central Columns

Above the squares written by family members are four squares written by Mary Susan Rice's friends (see grid pattern on figure 7). As in the family blessing unit, these four blocks can be read either horizontally or vertically and still relate to each other. Like a puzzle, they must have been arranged according to textual relatedness and then sewn into their respective columns. B–6 is a personal message similar to a letter. It advises Rice on how to use this quilt:

> I feel dear Susan that this memento of the love of your friends will prove a comfort to your spirit as well as body. When you wrap this gift about you, we'll feel that you are, as it were, enfolded in the arms of your friends and when your eyes meet our names may it be to you as a pledge, that we will never cease to bear you in the arms of faith and prayer before the throne of our Father in heaven from whence may blessings ever descend upon you.

Here is a clear statement concerning the dual purpose of this quilt. It was meant for warmth but it was also meant to be read.

Below this epistolary instruction is block C-6, the Mosaic prayer from the third book of Deuteronomy: "I pray let me go over and see the good land that is beyond the Jordan (Deut[eronomy] 3:25)." This is certainly a reference to Rice's plans to go over the Atlantic–a metaphorical Jordan. Next to this, still within the midline, is C-5–a verse from Proverbs: "A man's head deviseth his way, but the Lord directeth his steps." As well as continuing the imagery of movement found on C-6, this is direct Biblical support of that Congregational/Puritan philosophy that Rice would have encountered under Mary Lyon's tutelage at Mount Holyoke Seminary. Lyon said, "I verily believe that many things that God now designs to do he leaves to to be thought of by his children."[42] The way Rice chose to help accomplish God's design is found above C-5 on square B-5. This has Jesus' call to spread the gospel: "Go ye into the world and teach the gospel to every creature (Mat[thew] 28:19)."

Directly below the family blessing unit lie F-5, F-6, G-5, and G-6, another unit of friends' blocks that are inter-related. The suffering that everyone expected Rice to experience is alluded to in block F-5: "I reckon that the sufferings of this present time are not worthy to be compared with the glory which shall be revealed in us (Romans 8:18)." This block could refer up to the family unit, thus acknowledging the suffering Rice's family would endure without her. It could also refer to the suffering Rice might experience in Persia or to the suffering of Susan Shedd, the author of the poem written on F-6:

> Thus, then, in peace depart
> And angels guard thy footsteps.
> There is a feeling in the heart
> That will not let thee go.
> Yet go, thy spirit stays with me,
> Yet go, my spirit goes with thee.

Though this poem is rather sentimental, it is the most controlled and effective poem on the entire quilt. Susan Shedd, one of Mary Susan Rice's friends, felt the same anguish as Rice's family when thinking about the departure of her friend.

G-5 and G-6 continue the blessings of Rice's friends. Block G-6 is another friend's positive affirmation of Mary Susan Rice's momentous decision. This block contains the longest inscription on the quilt. Written on the bias of a three-inch square is a ninety-seven word message—a biblical passage from Isaiah which is followed by a personal message. Harriet Weston's choice continues the theme of the promise of God's protection while traveling over water.

Squares Bordering the Central Columns

Columns 3 and 4 and 7 and 8, both of which flank the two central columns 5 and 6, also have some inscriptions that relate to the messages from Rice's family and friends (see medium gray area of figure 7). As the reader of the quilt moves towards the outside edges, the squares are less closely related to each other but all have some reference to Rice's mission.

Columns 3 and 4 have blocks that are textually aligned with those in the midline. The Psalmic reassurance on D-3, "As the mountains are round about Jerusalem, so is the Lord round about his people" goes well with its neighbor from Deuteronomy on D-4: "the Lord thy God he doth go with thee, he will not fail thee." Both of these reinforce the family's blessing in the central columns; all give assurance that God will protect Rice all day and night.

Column 7 has been carefully aligned vertically with the midline columns. Rice's two sisters' squares on rows D and E of column 7 have already been mentioned; they form part of the family's blessing. The Bible verse on B-7 continues the theme of sleeping found in B-6 letter to Rice. The passage on C-7 is from Deuteronomy 31: "The Lord he it is that doth go before thee. He will be with thee, he will not fail thee." It follows logically that passage already cited on C-6–the Mosaic prayer about crossing the Jordan. C-7 is aligned horizontally with the promise penned on C-8 telling of hope for the eventual success of Jesus' disciples: "And they went forth and Preached everywhere, the Lord being with them and Working with them and confirming the word with signs following (Mark 16:20)."

Blocks D-8 and E-8 contain the only other poems on the top section. E-8's wish for Rice's success is sincere though stilted. Current issues show through the sentimentality of block D-8:

> For love of souls thou bravest the deep
> For love thou leavest dear kindred here
> Then will thou in thy memory keep
> Thy friends who for thee shed a tear.
> Thou will not forget when far away
> The heathen in thy native land
> Desire whenever thou kneelest to pray
> To meet them all at God's right hand.

The first verse continues the theme of going across the ocean and the sorrow of friends. The second verse has a cautionary note. There was an issue within the Sewing Circle regarding the support of domestic missions versus support of foreign missions.[43] This verse seems to imply that there is plenty of work still to be done in Rice's own country.

The scriptural passage on square E-8 also comes from that reassuring section of Isaiah: "Fear thou not; for I am thy God. Be not dismayed, for I am with thee (Isaiah 41:10)." In the same square follows a personal message: "We wish you in his name The most divine success, Assured that he who sends you forth Will your endeavor bless."

The Skirt Area

The quilt's skirt—those sections formed by the two cut-out corners—are rows A 1 and 2 through G 1 and 2, A 9 and 10 down to G 9 and 10, and rows H and I, 3 through 8. They would fall on the sides and bottom of the bed respectively and would be less likely to be seen and read with daily use (see light gray squares on figure 7). Many of these squares, whether personal messages or biblical quotations, reflect on the gravity of Mary Susan Rice's upcoming pilgrimage. Others contain only single names like that of Ellen A. Fiske on A-2, Caroline Whitney on I-8, or Louisa Wheeler on square E-10. Nine of the legible squares in the skirt area are signatures only—women who were members of the Sewing Circle and who wished to contribute to its construction. These squares with single names and those with formulaic sentiments such as "God Speed thee Friend" on I-6, "Be of Good Cheer" on A-10, and "When in that distant land, remember me." on D-10 seem less important to the quilt's overall message. This is probably why they were placed closer to the outside edges rather than the center of the quilt.

There are, however, some personal sentiments in the skirt area that show genuine anguish at the thought of the departure of a good friend. Though formulaic, Mary Edwards's poem on D-9 is such an example:

> Distant though our souls are blending
> Still my heart is warm and true.
> In my prayers to heaven ascending
> Sister, I'll remember you.
> Heaven preserve you,
> Safely on your journey through.

Eight of the blocks on the side skirts have passages from the Old Testament. Most reflect the need for trust, such as the choice from Psalm 56 on Square B-1. Another's choice on F-2 indicates her trust that God would keep Mary Susan Rice safe. B-10 states directly,

"Trust in the Lord and do good (Psalm 37)." These blocks are randomly interspersed with signature blocks and five blocks with selections from the New Testament, many of which praise Rice's motive in going. B-2 cites the familiar beatitude, "Blessed are the pure in heart for they shall see God." C-10 cautions, "For ye have need of patience, that, after ye have done the will of God, ye might receive the promise." Also in the skirt on G-9 is Matthew's direct call to mission: "Go ye therefore and teach all nations to love all things whatsoever I have commanded you."

Row A's First Block

Four of the nine squares in Row A are single signatures and a standardized farewell; the other five are more loosely related to the central columns; they cover the subjects of faith, rest, and fulfillment. This row would be less likely to be seen since it might be covered with pillows or a turned sheet. Even though block A-1 is in the top row and in the skirt area, I feel it is one of the most important squares on the whole quilt and centrally important in Mary Susan Rice's decision to leave her family and friends to serve in a foreign mission (see figure 8).The "Mary" on A-1 may be Mary Lyon, the founder and director of Mount Holyoke Female Seminary, the school Mary Susan Rice attended in 1846, the year before she decided to become a missionary in Persia. In order to better understand Rice's religious commitment to mission work, it is necessary to know something about Mount Holyoke and its founder, Mary Lyon.

Mount Holyoke Female Seminary

Mount Holyoke Female Seminary in Hadley, Massachusetts, was founded in 1837 almost single-handedly by Mary Lyon, a gifted teacher and pioneer in the area of education for women.[44] Mary Lyon, a committed Christian, "may have joined the Congregational Church because of its close association with the historical mainstream of Puritan tradition in America."[45] As a Congregationalist, she shared with the Puritans a belief in salvation through good works. Mary Lyon believed in the intervention of God into human affairs and taught her students that all of a person's wisdom would be needed to carry out God's purpose.[46]

Terms at Mount Holyoke were intense, both educationally, physically, and emotionally. All of the Holyoke seminarians were expected to help maintain the school as well as keep up with a strict regimen of study.[47] All students were exposed to Mary Lyon's revivals–quiet, personal experiences in which a woman professed her faith and was "saved."[48] By the end of 1846, when Mary Susan Rice was enrolled at Mount Holyoke, seventy-two of the ninety students experienced conversion.[49] Since Rice announced her intention to go to Persia in February of 1847, she must have been present at this successful revival.

All of her adult life, Mary Lyon was a faithful supporter of the American Board of Commissioners for Foreign Missions (ABCFM), "the largest and most influential American mission board in the early nineteenth century."[50] Lyon was acquainted with Ann Hasseltine, one of America's first women missionaries, who went to Burma with her husband in 1812.[51] Traditionally, in order for a woman to be accepted as a missionary by the ABCFM, she had to be married.[52]

Lyon was concerned with what her students would do after they left her seminary.[53] While she realized that most of them would marry, she did not discourage the call of her students to mission work since it offered them one of the best opportunities for usefulness–an active involvement in converting and perfecting the world.[54] By 1849 thirty-five graduates of Mount Hoyoke had become missionaries, most of them accompanying their missionary husbands.[55]

Fidelia Fiske, a graduate of and teacher at Mount Holyoke, was the first single woman the ABCFM accepted as a missionary.[56] In 1843, Fiske sailed from Boston as a missionary bound for Oroomiah, Persia. Mary Lyon showed her support for Fiske in this pioneering venture by traveling over a hundred miles from Hadley to Boston to see Fiske off.[57]

In 1847, Mary Susan Rice, also an unmarried Holyoke graduate, felt herself called to join Fidelia Fiske at the school Fiske referred to as the "Holyoke of Oroomiah."[58] Mary Lyon, who was not very well and was always burdened with the cares of teaching

Figure 10: The cross made out of Mary Lyon's hair, presented to Mary Susan Rice by Mary Lyon before Rice left for Persia in 1847. Found in the Mount Holyoke College Archives, Hadley, Massachusetts.

at and running Mount Holyoke, did not travel to Boston to see Rice off. But Lyon showed her approval of Rice's mission by sending Rice a cross made out of Lyon's own hair (see figure 10). Perhaps Rice asked Mary Lyon for a contribution that could be included on the Sewing Circle's quilt .

Written on square A-1 is the following Biblical verse and personal sentiment :

> For I the Lord thy God
> will hold thy right hand
> saying unto thee, fear not
> I will help thee.   Isa[iah] 41:13
> I can ask no greater blessing
> for my sister when in a
> heathen land than that
> the Lord may "hold her
> right hand"
>   Mary

Provenance of A-1

While there is no way to definitively prove that Mary Lyon was the author of square A-1, there are several clues that support the theory that the square is quite unusual. Though the writing on some nineteenth-century album quilts was done by one or two people considered to have the best handwriting, there are a wide variety of signatures on the missionary quilt.[59] The handwriting on square A-1 is unusual in that it appears to have been written by Mary Susan Rice herself. Similarities are apparent in a comparison of the handwriting on square A-1 with another sample of Rice's own handwriting (see figures 11 A and 11 B). Lyon could have sent Rice the inscription to transcribe onto a fabric square.

Square A-1 is unusual in another way. It is the only block on the entire quilt in which the fabric used in the horizontal brown sashing is also used in the construction of the Nine Patch (see figure 12). This suggests that A-1 may have been made into a Nine Patch either when the sashing was being added to the other eighty-one squares or was made by the person who contributed the brown sashing. If Rice received something from Lyon after the assembly of the quilt top had already begun, then the inscription on A-1 could not be added to those of central importance already in the middle of the quilt top, but could have been added later to the top on the outside strip of blocks.

The inscription itself, with the verse from Isaiah, is remarkably similar to Lyon's own statement that, "There were days in which I could not attempt any thing [sic] except to ask God to hold me by his own hand."[60] The square's personal message seems to be a restatement of Lyon's belief "of doing all we do because God would have it done."[61] The use of the first person singular and the phrase "heathen land" reiterate Lyon's devotion to the cause of foreign missions as a way to bring the entire world to the cause of Christ. It is a prayer and blessing which parallels Lyon's advice to her students to, "Pray for yourself as an individual—What does God require of you . . . in relation to the heathen world? What do we need from God that he may do what he requires of us." [62]

Whoever the Mary was, the message on A-1 reflects the long message from Harriet Weston on block G-6; both selections from Isaiah are almost sequential. Together they bracket and synthesize

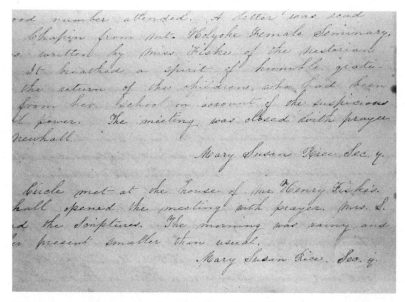

Figure 11 A: Sample of the handwriting of Mary Susan Rice as found in the minutes of the Sewing Circle. Photograph by author.

Figure 11 B: Detail of the handwriting on square A-1. Photograph by author.

Figure 12: Detail of square A-1 showing the brown sashing that is also used in the construction of the Nine Patch. Photograph by author.

a message that Mary Susan Rice would need always to remember–
that no matter what happened to her, she should not be afraid. She
had God's promise that he would be with her as she carried out his
plan. Certainly, Mary Susan Rice would have cherished a memento
from this extraordinary leader in education for women–the person
who inspired Mary Susan Rice in this daring, altruistic enterprise–
an enterprise that would itself involve education of women.

Mary Susan Rice's "Divine Success"

Mary Susan Rice's missionary enterprise had mixed results. It was
successful in that she did not die in Persia and remained there for
twenty-two years. She helped implement progressive ideas about
the role of women in a society where women were not educated
and considered second-class citizens.[63] She was able to help Nestorian women learn "to read and write and to expect companion-
ship in marriage."[64] She witnessed the conversion of some of her
students in Holyoke-type revivals.[65] She and her colleagues in
Oroomiah "were deeply impressed by their students' eagerness to
please and be good Christians, and by their affection."[66]

Mary Susan Rice also suffered some incredible hardships. Over
the years she saw her students and colleagues die from a variety of
illnesses like measles, "Influenza, which is prevailing as an epi-
demic," and cholera.[67] She herself severely injured her ankle and
may have been bothered by it for the rest of her life.[68] By 1866, the
minutes of the Sewing Circle state that "letters from Mary Susan
Rice [indicate that] her health is failing."[69]

The very presence of the Christian missionaries in Oroomiah
exacerbated the civil conflicts between the Kurds and Muslims and
the Nestorians who, as one of the earliest Christian sects, had lived
peacefully with other faiths until the arrival of the missionaries.[70]
The missionaries' presence, directed at the preexisting Christians,
actually hurt these Christian Persians of whom the other native
peoples were jealous. Rice was probably not aware of the long-
term negative effect of her well-intentioned vocation.

Her immediate assessment of what the missionaries were accom-
plishing was often very enthusiastic. She wrote to a friend in 1849:

We, in foreign lands are encouraged,
to know that Christians at home and
Christians abroad love this day, and love
to pray for those on mission ground. May
they pray on and on, till the dark portions
of the earth are filled with the glory of Emmanuel.[71]

Undoubtedly, this is the same sort of sentiment she wrote in her letters that were read out loud in the monthly meetings of the Lincoln Missionary Sewing Circle: "The afternoon was pleasantly spent in plying the busy needle, social chat and listening to a number of letters from Miss S. Rice."[72]

The Circle continued to make other quilts after Rice left for Persia. In 1855 the secretary noted, "Not withstanding the oppressive heat, about sixty assembled . . . . A quilt which was put in the frames in the morning, was nearly finished."[73] Up until the Civil War the quilts that the Circle made continued to be sold at the December fairs to help support missionaries like their own Mary Susan Rice; but there is no record of their sending off another quilt with a particular missionary.

In 1869, Mary Susan Rice came back with her quilt to her beloved Lincoln, Massachusetts. The minutes document a large turnout in September 1869 because Rice would be present.[74] A few months after her return, Rice "encourage[d] the circle in her field of labor, particularly Jessamen, the pupil, who has been supported by [a] Lincoln . . . school." [75] It is unclear whether this Nestorian student was in the United States or in Persia. The Circle may have helped the Persian student, but the general policy of the Sewing Circle had changed. It turned its attention away from foreign missions and concentrated almost exclusively in supporting home missions.

Mary Susan Rice returned to the same home (the Hunt-Rice Tavern) about which she wrote so wistfully on the Catalpa twenty-two years earlier. There is little information about the rest of Rice's life. According to her descendants, after her parents' home was sold, she lived with one of her sisters for the rest of her life. Periodic references in the records of the Sewing Circle give brief glimpses of her. Chronic ill health certainly would explain her absence from the Sewing Circle from 1870 to 1880. Perhaps she was also disappointed in the Sewing Circle's change of focus which may have seemed a negation of her two prior decades of work.

In 1880, Rice is again mentioned as taking part in the monthly meetings. She must have personally kept in touch with her Persian colleagues, since in January 1881 she read a letter "giving an account of the siege of Oroomiah."[76] She may have started to travel again since her photograph in fashions of the 1890s was taken in Washington, D.C. (see figure 3).[77]

By 1903 Mary Susan Rice is mentioned as an honorary member of the Sewing Circle.[78] When she died in 1905, the following tribute was entered in the minutes: "when no longer able to help in any other way, her prayers for all God's work in her beloved church continued. . . . Though she has passed from us the influence of her life and prayers . . . remains with us and acts as an incentive to greater efforts."[79]

Conclusion

The comparison of Mary Susan Rice's missionary album quilt with other album quilts made in New England towns during the 1840s and 1850s confirms that many were made according to a certain formula then in vogue. The Lincoln Missionary Sewing Circle's treatment of this regional album formula resulted in a quilt that was not formulaic. The poems, letters, and biblical passages preserved on Mary Susan Rice's missionary album quilt reveal a history of a group of nineteenth-century women as complex as the arrangement of the blocks in the quilt top.

At a time when most women's lives revolved only around their homes, Mary Susan Rice made a heroic, independent stand and left all she knew for an ideal thousands of miles away. The missionary quilt she took with her testifies to the Sewing Circle's affection for Rice and also shows the members' tacit support for Rice's daring venture. The fact that the quilt traveled with Rice to Persia and back, was carefully conserved, and left to her relatives shows the quilt's importance to Mary Susan Rice. The quilt's varied inscriptions must have been as one square says, "a comfort to [her] spirit as well as body."

Acknowledgments

This paper could not have been written without the generous encouragement of the owners of Mary Susan Rice's quilt, Jerry Cirillo and the staff of the wonderful Lincoln, Massachusetts, Public Library, and Patricia J. Albright, Archives Librarian at Mount Holyoke College in Hadley, Massachusetts.

Notes and References

1. All quotes are taken from one of two unpublished journals kept by Mary Susan Rice when she was a missionary in Persia from 1847 until 1869. The journals are privately owned by one of her descendants, a resident of Lincoln, Massachusetts. Unless otherwise noted, the author will cite Rice with only the date of the journal entry.

2. Rice, *Journal*, June 1847.

3. John MacLean, *A Rich Harvest* (Lincoln, MA: The Lincoln Historical Society, 1988), 369–71. MacLean noted that The Liberal School, a private institution started in Lincoln in the eighteenth century, set a precedent for advances in women's education for Lincoln's public schools.

4. By a Lady [Elizabeth Farrar], *The Young Lady's Friend* (Boston: American Stationers' Co., 1837), 2.

5. *Ninth Annual Catalog of Mount Holyoke Female Seminary* (Amherst, MA : J.S. and C. Adams, 1846). Available at the Mount Holyoke College Archives and Special Collections, Mount Holyoke College, South Hadley, Massachusetts.

6. *The New Pictorial Family Magazine*, ed. Robert Sears (New York: Robert Sears Publishing, 1847), 322.

7. *Ninth Annual Catalog of Mount Holyoke Female Seminary.*

8. Amanda Porterfield, *Mary Lyon and the Mount Holyoke Missionaries* (New York: Oxford University Press, 1997), 74.

9. Rice, *Journal*, 15 August 1847.

10. A Returned Missionary [Thomas Laurie], *Woman and Her Savior in Persia* (Boston: Gould and Lincoln, 1863), 37.

11. Rice, *Journal*, 29 July 1847. Mary G. may be Mary Gross, a member of the Lincoln Missionary Sewing Circle.

12. Elizabeth A. Green, *Mary Lyon and Mount Holyoke: Opening the Gates* (Hanover, NH: University Press of New England, 1979), 260.

13. Rice, *Journal*, 31 July 1847.

14. Mary Susan Rice's quilt is privately owned by one of her descendents who lives in Lincoln, Massachusetts.

15. MacLean, 381.

16. *Records of the Female Missionary Sewing Circle of Lincoln. 1842–1863*, III-1, Archives of Lincoln, Massachusetts, Public Library, June 1842.
17. Ibid., April 1850.
18. Ibid., July 1843.
19. Ibid., September 1843.
20. Ibid., November 1843.
21. Ibid., June 1846.
22. Though the author, Elizabeth Farrar, was listed as one of the founding members of the Sewing Circle, Mrs. Dorcas Farrar was the purchaser of the quilt. Dorcas Farrar may have been the sister-in-law of Elizabeth Farrar.
23. *Records*, III-1, March 1847.
24. Jeanette Lasansky, "T-Shaped Quilts; A New England Phenomenon," *The Magazine Antiques*, December 1997, 842–45.
25. Linda Otto Lipsett, *Remember Me. Women and their Friendship Quilts* (San Francisco: Quilt Digest Press, 1985), 25.
26. Jacqueline Marx Atkins, *Shared Threads*, (New York: Museum of American Folk Art, 1994), 38.
27. Ibid.
28. Lipsett, 21.
29. The dominant patterns used on New England album quilts during this period were Nine Patch, Cross Ties (Album Cross), and Chimney Sweep, all of which have a central area suitable for signatures.
30. For examples of other New England album quilts made in the fourth and fifth decades of the nineteenth century, see: Linda Otto Lippsett *To Love and to Cherish* (San Francisco CA: Quilt Digest Press, 1989), 93, 100; Ricky Clark, "Fragile Families Quilts As Kinship Bonds," *Quilt Digest*, Volume 5, ed. Michael M. Kile (San Francisco, CA: Quilt Digest Press, 1989), 8; Richard L. Cleveland and Donna Bister, *Plain and Fancy* (San Francisco, CA: Quilt Digest Press, 1991), 63; Robert J. Schleck, *The Wilcox Quilts in Hawaii* Kuaui, Hawaii: Grove Farm Homestead and Waioli Mission House, 1986), 16; Jean Ray Laury and the California Quilt Project, *Ho for California* (New York: E. F. Dutton, 1990), 37, 48; Linda Otto Lipsett, *Remember Me*, 22, 31, 34, 63, 72, 100; E. Duane Elbert and Rachel Kamm Elbert, *History from the Heart* (Nashville, TN: Rutledge Hill Press, 1993), 34; Victoria Hoffman, *Quilts: A Window To the Past* (North Andover, MA: Museum of American Textile History, 1991), 6; *The Great American Coverup: Counterpanes of the 18th and 19th Centuries* (Baltimore, MD: Baltimore Museum of Art, 1971), 18, 30.
31. Though this tiny album quilt top is not dated, its owner, Vivian Sayer, quilt appraiser and lecturer, has determined from the fabrics that it was made in the 1840s. It has all of the characteristics of other album quilts made in New England in the second quarter of the nineteenth century.
32. Ricky Clark, "Quilt Documentation: A Case Study," in *Making the Amer-*

ican Home: Middle Class Women and Domestic Material Culture 1840–1940, ed. Marilyn Ferris Motz and Pat Browne (Bowling Green, OH: Bowling Green State University Press, 1988), 113.

33. Ibid., 179–82. In her study of an Ohio quilt, Ricky Clark noted the deliberate assemblage of inscribed squares into meaningful units. The Ohio quilt was made in the same decade as Rice's quilt.
34. Green, 266.
35. Henry Rice seems to have been a man with many interests. It must have been Rice who hired Rufus Porter to paint the murals on the walls of the Hunt-Rice Tavern. Under his ownership, the tavern was an important gathering spot for town residents; town meetings were often held there (MacLean, *A Rich Harvest*, 347). He was a member of the Lincoln Lyceum, an organization in which men heard lectures on and debated important historical and current subjects; one of those subjects was the importance of education for women (MacLean, 389). Since the First Parish Church was across from Henry Rice's tavern and since Mary Susan Rice was so involved in this religious organization, it is probable that her father was just as involved as she.
36. Green, 261.
37. Ibid.
38. Ibid.
39. *Records of the Missionary Sewing Circle of Lincoln, 1864–1885*, III-2, Archives of the Lincoln Public Library, Lincoln, MA, September 1869.
40. Rice, *Journal*, 13 August 1847.
41. Ibid., 23 August 1847.
42. Fidelia Fiske, *Recollections of Mary Lyon with selections from her instructions to the pupils of Mount Holyoke Female Seminary* (Boston: American Tract Society, 1866; reprint, Los Olivos, CA: Olive Press Publications, 1995), 108 (page references are to reprint edition).
43. *Records of the Missionary Sewing Circle*, III-1, January 1845.
44. Sara D. Locke Stow, *History of Mount Holyoke Seminary, South Hadley, Massachusetts during its first half century* (Springfield, MA: Springfield Printing Co., 1887), 84.
45. Porterfield, 74.
46. Ibid.
47. Fiske, 108.
48. Lisa Natale Drakeman, "Seminary Sisters: Mount Holyoke's first students, 1837–1849" (thesis, Princeton University, 1988), 122.
49. Ibid., 143.
50. Porterfield, 5.
51. Green, 27.
52. Ibid., 261.
53. Ibid.
54. Drakeman, 195.

55. Green, 264.
56. Ibid., 242.
57. Ibid.
58. Porterfield, 68.
59. Atkins, 37.
60. Fiske, 139.
61. Ibid., 220.
62. Ibid., 176.
63. Porterfield, 68.
64. Ibid.
65. Ibid., 73.
66. Ibid.
67. Rice, *Journal,* 19 January 1848.
68. Mary Susan Rice to Sarah Packard, August 1864, Archives and Special Collections, Mount Holyoke College, South Hadley, MA.
69. *Records Of Missionary Sewing Circle,* III-2, October 1866.
70. Porterfield, 81.
71. Mary Susan Rice to Susanna Fitch, 19 December 1849, Archives and Special Collections, Mount Holyoke College, South Hadley, MA.
72. *Records of the Missionary Sewing Circle,* III-1, April 1851.
73. Ibid., September 1855.
74. *Records,* III-2, September 1869.
75. Ibid., December 1869.
76. Ibid., January 1881.
77. Virginia Gunn notes that since fashion changed almost annually, Mary Susan Rice's photograph can be narrowed fairly accurately to ca. 1895.
78. *Records of the Missionary Sewing Circle of Lincoln, 1886–1907,* III-3. January 1903.
79. Ibid., June 1905.

Appendix
Messages Written on Mary Susan Rice's Quilt.

A-1 For I the Lord thy God / Will hold thy right hand, / Saying unto thee fear not, / I will help thee (Isa[iah] 41:13). I can ask no greater thing / for my sister, when in a / heathen land, then that / the Lord may "hold her right hand." Mary

A-2 Ellen A. Fiske

A-3 My praise shall go with / thee and I will give thee rest Ex[odus] 33:14 .

A-4 Lo, everyone that thirsteth / come ye to the waters, and he / that hath no money, come ye / buy and eat; yea, come, buy / wine and milk without / money and and without price Lucy H. Store (Isa[iah] 55:1)

A-5   Thou wilt keep him in / perfect peace whose mind / is stayed on thee because / he trusteth in thee. Mary Flagg Isa[iah] 26:3

A–6   I live by the faith of the son of God. Lucy Ames Gal[atians] 2:20.

A-7   The Lord is my / Shepherd. I shall / not want. Susan Parker Martha Parker.

A-8   Im [?] da Gould. March 20th 47.

A-9   Sarah Fiske

A-10 Be of good cheer. Abigail Smith

B-1   "In God I will praise his word / in God I have put my trust; / I will not fear what flesh can / do unto me." Sarah Colburn.

B-2   Blessed are the pure / in heart for they / shall see God . Matt. V:8. Lucy Hartwell.

B-3   Malachi 4: 2. But unto you that fear / my name shall the Sun / of Righteousness arise. Abby W. Fiske.

B-4   All go unto one place / All are of the dust and / All turn to dust again Susan Parks (Gen[esis] 3:14)

B-5   Go ye unto / the world, / and teach the / gospel / to every creature. Mary F. _____

B-6   I feel, dear Susan, that this memento / of the love of your friends, will prove a / comfort to your spirit, as well as body. When you wrap this gift about / you, will feel that you are, as it were, / enfolded in the arms of . your friends / and when your eyes meet our names / may it be to you as a pledge, that we will never cease to bear you in / the arms of faith and prayer, before / the throne of our Father in heaven, from whence may blessings ever / descend upon you.

B-7   When thou liest down thou / shalt not be afraid, yea, thou shalt lie down and thy sleep shall be sweet for the Lord shall be thy confidence, / and shall keep thy foot from being taken. (Prov[erbs] 3: 22, 26) Mary Edwards.

B-8   Is[aiah]33: 4 For the word of the Lord / _____ and all his works / he does in truth. Susan M. Fiske.

B-9   Be of good / courage and he shall strengthen / your heart. (Psalms 27:14) L. W. Bemis .

B-10 Trust in the Lord and / do good. (Psalm 37: 3) Abby Colburn.

C-1   Be not afraid / only believe. J. A. Bemis.

C-2   Submit T_____ulier. April 13, 1847.

C-3   Remember me. Caroline Smith

C-4   Let this banner / over her / be _____. Mary Flag

C-5   A man's heart / deviseth his way / but the Lord directeth / his steps. (Prov[erbs]16:9) Susan Park. April 12, 1847.

C-6   I pray let me go over and / see the good land that is beyond Jordan. (Deut[eronomy] 3:25.

C-7 The Lord he it is that doth / go before thee: He will be with thee, he will not fail thee, neither forsake thee / fear not, neither be dismayed (Deut[eronomy] 31: 8) Mary Billings.

C-8 And they went forth, and / Preached everywhere, the Lord / Working with them, and confirming / the word with signs following. Eveline Wheeler. (Mark 16:20).

C-9 God having provided / some better things for us that they with / out us should not be made perfect. (Heb[rews] XI: 40) . Louisa Hartwell.

C-10 For ye have need of patience, that, after ye have done the will of God / ye might receive the promise. Heb[rews] 10 36. E. L. P. Stone

D-1 (Indiscipherable).

D-2 Let them give glory / unto the Lord and / declare his praise in / the islands. (Is[aiah]. 42:12). Lucy Stone.

D-3 As the mountains are round about Jerusalem, / so is the Lord round about / his people from hence forth even forever more. (Ps[alms] 123:2) Mary Flint

D-4 Be strong and of good courage / for the Lord thy God, he it is that doth go with thee, he will not fail thee nor forsake thee. Elizabeth F. Wheeler. [Deuteronomy 31:6] Lincoln, April 13, 1847

D-5 Behold, he that keepeth / Israel, shall neither / slumber nor sleep. The Lord is thy keeper. (Ps[alms]121:45) Caroline A. Rice.

D-6 The Lord bless thee and keep thee. The Lord lift up his / countenance upon thee and give thee peace. (Num[bers] 6:24, 26) Susanna Sherburne

D-7 Trust ye in the Lord forever, for in the Lord Jehovah is everlasting strength. (Is[aiah] 26: 4) S. Catherine Rice.

D-8 For love of souls thou bravest the deep, / For love thou leavest dear kindred here, / Then will thou in thy memory keep / The friends who for thee shed a tear. Thou will not forget when far away, The heathen in thy native land, / Desire, whenever thou kneelest to pray, / To meet them all at God's right hand. 1847. Abigail M. Wheeler

D-9 Distant though our souls are blending, / Still my heart is warm and true; / In my prayers to heaven ascending / Sister–I'll remember you; / Heaven preserve you, / Safely on your journey through. Lincoln. March. 1847. Mary Edwards

D-10 When in that distant / land, remember me. Augusta Watts.

E-1 A_____. March 19, 1847

E-2 Martha S Brooks

E-3 I am not ashamed / of the gospel of Christ. (Rom[ans] 1:16) Lucy Fiske.

E-4 The eyes of the Lord are / over the righteous and his / ears are open unto their / prayers. Adaline A. Billings (Peter 3:12).

E-5 Go ye into all the world / and preach the gospel to / every creature. (Mark 16:15) James Rice

E-6   Father to thee / I yield the trust. O bless her with a love / Deeper and purer stronger far than mine. / Shield her from sin, from sorrow and from pain. / But should thy wisdom deem affliction best, / Let love be mingled with the chastening. / With an unshrinking heart I give her, Lord, to thee. / "Thy will not mine be done." Mary Rice.

E-7   There shall be no night there; / and they need no candle, / neither light of the sun, / for the Lord God giveth them / light; and they shall reign / for ever and ever. (Rev[elations] 22: 5). Louisa Rice.

E-8   Fear thou not; for I am thy God: / be not dismayed for I am with thee. (Isaiah 41:10). We wish you in his name, / The most divine success; / Assured that he who sends you forth, / Will your endeavor bless. Eliz. Wheeler. Lincoln, April 1847.

E-9   (John 17:20) Neither pray I nor thee / alone, but for them also / which shall believe / on me through the truth. Marcia Fiske

E-10   Louisa Wheeler

F-1   The righteous shall be in everlasting remembrance. (Ps[alms] 112: 6) Ellen Hartwell

F-2   The Lord shall preserve thy / going out and thy coming / in, from this time forth / and even for evermore. (Ps[alms]121: 8) Lydia Billings.

F-3   God is my salvation; I will / trust, and not be afraid. (Isaiah 12:2) Mary L. Ames

F-4   Blessed are they that / mourn: for they shall / be comforted. (Matt[hew] V:4) Abigail Flint.

F-5   I reckon that the sufferings / of this present time are not / [worthy to be compared] with the glory which shall be revealed in us. (Rom[ans]8:18) May the Lord watch [over us when we are] absent one from another. Lydia Flint.

F-6   Thus, then, in peace depart / And angels guard thy footsteps. / There is a feeling in the heart / That will not let thee go. / Yet go, thy spirit stays with me; / Yet go, my spirit goes with thee. Susan G. Shedd.

F-7   "He being dead / yet speaketh." (Heb[rews]11:4). Mary Flint.

F-8   And the spirit and / the bride say Come and / Let him that heareth say Come / And let him that is thirsty come / And whosoever will try him take the water of life freely.(Rev[elations] 22:17). So long as this text endures may / the smile of its Heavenly author / gladden the heart and [cheer] the pathway of Mary Susan, / most sincerely wish ___ Abby____

F-9   Lead me in thy truth / and teach me Ellen F. Colburn. [Psalm 25:5]

F-10   Indulgent God, to thee we pray; / Be with us on this solemn day; Our sister bless, her zeal approve / That zeal which burns to spread thy love. / With cheerful steps may she proceed / Where'er thy providence shall lead; Let heaven and earth her work befriend / And mercy all her [faith] attend. Nancy Smith

G-1   Martha Smith. April 1847.

G-2   "O Lord, open thou my lips / and my mouth shall show forth / thy
       praise." Harriet Colburn. (Psalm 51:15)

G-3   (2 Thes[solonians]8:16) "Now the Lord of peace / Give you peace
       always." Martha Fiske.

G-4   [Illegible]

G-5   Farewell, dear friend, / may heaven's blessings rest / upon you is the
       sincere prayer of / Priscilla Hagar.

G-6   Fear not; / for I have / redeemed thee, / I have called thee / by thy name;
       thou art / mine. When thou passeth / through the waves I will be / with
       thee; and through the rivers / They shall not overflow thee. When / thou
       walkest through the fire thou / shall not be burned, neither shall the /
       flame kindle upon thee. For I am the Lord / thy God, the Holy One of
       Israel, thy Savior. (Isaiah 43:1–3). That the promise of the presence of
       the / Holy One be continually realized / by my precious friend, through /
       all her pilgrimage here below is the prayer of / H. G. Weston.

G-7   Be strong / Let not your hands be weak / For your works shall / be
       rewarded. (II Chron[icals]. 15:7). Susan Flint.

G-8   (1 Peter 5:7) "Cast all your care upon him / for he careth for you." Mary
       N. Russell.

G-9   Go ye therefore and / teach all nations to love / all things whatsoever, I
       have / commanded you. and lo, I am / with you always even unto the
       end / of the world. (Matt[hew] 28:18). Elizabeth Hardy

G-10   Verily, I say unto where / soever this gospel shall be _____ ed through-
       out the whole world. / This also that she hath done shall be spoken of for
       a memorial of her. Sarah Dukin

H-3   Peace be within thy walls [and prosperity within thy palaces]. (Ps[alms]
       122:7). Ellen Wheeler

H-4   Trust in the Lord / And do good / and verily thou / shall be fed. (Ps[alms]
       37:3). S. C. Hagar.

H-5   God bless the missionary. Susan D.Brooks.

H-6   Ye shall go out with joy / and be led forth with peace / the mountains and
       the hills / shall break forth before you / into singing and all the _____ of
       the field shall / clap their hands (Isa[iah] 55:12). Edith L. P. Stone.

H-7   I the Lord have called / thee in righteousness, and / will hold thine
       hand, / and will keep thee. (Isa[iah] 42:6). Francis Flint.

H-8   And let us not be weary / in well doing: for in / due season we shall / reap
       if we faint not. (Gal[atians] 6:9). Dorcas Farrar

I-3   Sarah Whitney.

I-4   I will not leave you comfort- / less; I will come to you. (_____XIV:18). Lo

I am with you always, / even unto the end of the world. (Matt[hew] XXVIII:20). Mary Ann Hartwell.

I-5　God speed thee friend Caroline S. Benjamin

I-6　But the fruit of the / Spirit is love, joy, / peace, long suffering, / gentleness, goodness, / faith. (Gal[atians] 5:22). Dorcas Farrar

I-7　The love of Christ _____ us Elizabeth H. ____dale.

I-8　Caroline Whitney

Learning to Quilt
with Grandma Mary Sibley:
Gift Labor, Traditional Quiltmaking,
and Contemporary Art

Heather Lenz

Mary Sibley, born in 1916, has created and hand-quilted nearly two hundred quilts since her retirement at the age of sixty-five. Sibley typically gives her quilts away as soon as they are completed; most remain within the extended family. The author of this essay, Heather Lenz, is Sibley's granddaughter. In college Lenz studied art history and sculpture within a dominant paradigm: fine arts (painting and sculpture) are superior to crafts (glassblowing and metalsmithing); quiltmaking ranks even lower, a skill in which a legitimate degree cannot be earned.

During quilting lessons with her grandmother, Lenz learns from Sibley's wisdom, perseverance, and generosity and is opened up to a gentler paradigm which revolves around gift labor. In addition, Sibley's traditional quiltmaking is contrasted with the work of established contemporary female artists; parallels become obvious. Methods include: oral history, field study, and an analysis of critical writings on contemporary art.

"You can be worried about this, or that, or the other thing, but when you start to make a quilt, the only thing you worry about is finishing that quilt."[1]
  —Mary Sibley

It is a typical morning in mid-November 1994. Grandma Sibley rises early, at 6:00 A.M. She turns on the news and after a quick breakfast of toast and coffee she sits at her quilting frame and begins the process of moving the needle in and out, through the fabric. "I'm a morning person," she often tells me; "I can get more done in the morning than any other time of day."[2]

One hundred and fifty miles away, my day unfolds. At 6:00 A.M., I am leaving the sculpture studio after a night of pouring hot wax into plaster molds. For the last several weeks I have been casting large, pink tongues as part of a sculpture later entitled "Silent," about stifled speech. I am working on my senior show, the body of work I need to complete in order to graduate. I am twenty-four and live in Akron, Ohio. My grandmother is seventy-nine and resides in Clymer, Pennsylvania (see figure 1).

At 10:30 A.M., Grandma stops quilting and takes a short break to get lunch going. Her keen color sense carries over into meal-making. "If it looks good, it tastes good," she comments, during one of my visits, as she places certain vegetables next to others, "for color."[3] She returns to her quilting frame until noon when she stops to eat. Afterwards, she reads the day's mail, then threads her sewing machine and begins piecing another new quilt.

Following a few early morning hours of sleep, I eat a late breakfast and turn to my thesis, which requires a detailed discussion of my sculptures. I am struggling; reading publications like *Art Forum* and *Art in America*, I feel overwhelmed. Phrases like *the post-conceptual, political, tableau,* and *mechanic, hermetic, theorization* are everywhere and I realize for the first time that this language is not used exclusively by the critics but by the artists themselves. A Kiki Smith interview with Robin Winters comforts me. In the article Smith states, "I don't have a strategy. I am not working out of an agenda. For me there is no difference between living and doing my work—there's no separation . . . basically it's just what occurs to me."[4]

By mid-afternoon the sewing machine is hot and Grandma takes another break. She works on a crossword puzzle, decides what to eat for dinner, and begins meal preparation. Then she sews for a few more hours, interrupted every so often by neighbors who drop by to visit. There are compliments about the inviting aroma coming from the kitchen. When her dinner is ready she stops sewing and eats while watching the evening news. After washing the dishes she continues working into the evening. Eight to ten hours of quiltmaking per day is common.

Figure 1. Photograph of Mary Sibley by her grandson, Gus (R. Augustus Powell), 1994.

Meanwhile, I grab dinner at Taco Bell and return to the sculpture studio. Next I plug in a hot plate and begin to chisel large blocks of wax into more manageable pieces that fit inside my double boiler. The wax will take about an hour to melt; I stir it while working on my paper. With my oil paints I mix a dark red to pigment the wax; the color will be lighter when the wax cools again. It is dark out, past eleven. Earlier in the day I made clay, now I pack it against the seams of my three plaster molds and pour in the wax. Fortunately, there are no leaks, so I roll the molds along the floor to release air bubbles and distribute the contents evenly. Finally, I place the molds in a sink filled with cool water and crack them open.

≈

In art school I have been exposed to a dominant paradigm: *real art* is the slick stuff you see in the latest glossy issues of contemporary arts magazines; fine arts (painting, sculpture, and printmaking) are superior to crafts (glass blowing, metalsmithing, and weaving).

Quiltmaking ranks even lower, a skill in which a legitimate degree cannot be earned.

Visits to my grandmother expose me to a distinctly contrary paradigm, in which the value of gift labor outweighs the most expensive fine art. In her essay, "The Viewer, the Sitter, and the Site: A Splintered Syntax," art critic, Lynne Cooke states, "gift economies knit individuals into a larger context, a community."[5] In his book, *The Gift: Imagination and the Erotic Life of Property*, philosopher Lewis Hyde expounds, "It is the cardinal difference between gift and commodity exchange that a gift establishes a feeling-bond between two people, while the sale of a commodity leaves no necessary connection."[6]

My grandmother had been making and giving away quilts for years before I really began to understand the depths of her generosity and the intensity of her labor. In some of my earliest memories she sits at the sewing machine, hemming pants for a friend, making a wedding dress for a neighbor, or creating cushions for a freshly reupholstered sofa. But it was not until she started giving me sewing lessons that I truly appreciated the level of her skill. My own attempts to sew frequently ended in tangled thread and a jammed machine. Regardless, in the fall of 1993 we started working on our first quilt together, a star pattern called Chips and Whetstones (see figure 2).

"Now we're cooking with oil," my grandmother commented.[7] The pieces were finally going together smoothly, and I was relieved. Periodically, Grandma coaxed the fabric with, "You get in there little Missy," or sometimes, "little Bessy."[8] Each of the twelve stars in the Chips and Whetstones pattern consists of 184 pieces. Grandma gently accused me of picking the hardest design I could find. The difficulty she was experiencing in piecing the numerous, triangular shapes was largely the result of my choice of fabrics, and the way I cut the pieces. Still a novice at sewing, I did not understand the importance of cutting with the grain. To further complicate matters, the pieces had been cut from cottons, silks, and velvets.

During a previous visit, in the summer of 1993, Grandma had invited me to select scraps from a couple of boxes she kept in the closet. Many of the fabrics I chose were passed on to my grandmother from her daughter, Jeannie (Joan Sibley-Powell), who had once worked as a fashion designer in New York City.[9] The

Figure 2. Chips and Whetstones, 84" x 105", 1993–1994. Colors: background is navy blue cotton; strips of dark red velvet separate the multicolored stars. Sewn and quilted by Mary Sibley. (Pieces cut by the author.) Collection of the author. Photograph by Dennis Ryan.

high quality of the fabrics and the unusual designs on the scraps, many of which were decades old, appealed to me. A few months after I selected the fabrics, in October of 1993, Jeannie passed away, and my selections took on a greater poignancy. As Grandma and I worked on the quilt, the fabrics we were handling sometimes brought Grandma memories of her daughter, and she would tell me, "Jeannie used to make ties out of this fabric," or "Jeannie made a skirt out of this."[10] As another reminder of my seamstress aunt, I added a remnant of cotton printed with tiny scissors, dress forms, and flowers to the in-progress quilt.

Grandma and I worked together on the quilt during weekend visits and school breaks for over a year. We fell into a routine. I cut and arranged the pieces, then handed them to Grandma who attached them with the mechanical whir of the sewing machine. Long silences were common as we concentrated on our tasks. Occasionally Grandma would give me advice on how to cut multiple layers of fabric with a single swipe of the rotary cutter, or caution me against cutting my *pazucy* [Polish for fingers].[11] Other times she fondly recounted working on quilts with her daughter, Jeannie. "Sometimes she would intentionally cut the pieces too big or too small," Grandma recalled. In this way Jeannie hoped to mimic the sometimes irregular appearance of old quilts made entirely by hand. Despite Jeannie's training and her attention to detail in the creation of high-end, sometimes one-of-a-kind garments, in quilts she enjoyed the clearly handmade and preferred stitches she could really "see" to the extremely small, regular stitches so many quilters prize. Every now and then Grandma has commented, "I should have started quilting sooner, when I was younger, and my hands would have allowed me to make the small stitches," but then she remembers that Jeannie liked her stitches exactly as she made them.[12]

During other sewing sessions I learned that Jeannie liked to select dark calicos with small white prints, such as the black fabric with the tiny white flowers from which her Drunkard's Path was made (see figure 3). "The white flecks make the quilt sparkle," Jeannie used to tell her mother.[13] This piece of information would later influence my choice of fabrics for two of the quilts Grandma and I worked on together in 1997, the Pickle Dish and Turkey Tracks (see figure 4).

Figure 3. Drunkard's Path, 91" x 105", circa 1988. Colors: black and white. Made by Mary Sibley for her daughter, Jeannie (Sibley) Powell. Collection of Peter Powell and Gus Powell. Photograph by Dennis Ryan.

Throughout the year that Grandma and I worked on the Chips and Whetstones quilt, she also worked alone on several others. One of the quilts she made was linen with a large heart drawn in the center by using a stencil. The fabric came from a box under Jeannie's bed, which was mailed to Grandma at her request. Jeannie had told Grandma about the box of fabric during the year she

Figure 4. Pickle Dish, 84" x 103", 1996–1997. Colors: hunter green and white. Sewn and quilted by Mary Sibley with assistance from the author. (Pieces cut by the author.) Collection of the author. Photograph by Dennis Ryan.

struggled with lymphoma. She was redecorating her bedroom and hoped her mother would make her a new quilt with the fabric. Grandma was determined to finish the quilt despite her daughter's untimely death.[14] Always thinking about the next stitch helped her get through that difficult time. She later told me, "If it weren't for quiltmaking, I wouldn't have made it through."[15]

During the year of 1994, my mother, Nancy (Sibley) Lenz, spoke of her sister Jeannie often. In particular, she mentioned her sister's desire to document Grandma's wonderful quilts. As I continued to study contemporary art in college, this unfinished family project remained on my mind.

In May of 1995, I graduated after completing the required thesis and sculptures for my senior show. For the next six months I continued to make three-dimensional objects. Simultaneously, I found myself wanting to spend more and more time with my grandmother in her quiet one-bedroom apartment in rural Clymer, Pennsylvania; I wanted to learn the art of quiltmaking. I began visiting my grandmother frequently, usually one week out of every month. "You can be worried about this, or that, or the other thing," she told me, "but when you start to make a quilt, the only thing you worry about is finishing that quilt."[16] I was beginning to learn from my grandmother's focus and concentration, her busy hands and meditative approach to quilting.

The sculptures I made after graduation were less intuitive and more conceptual. I found myself wanting to determine in advance how the pieces I made could be interpreted with language; in this way I hoped to avoid the recent struggle I had faced discussing the artwork in my senior show. The sculptures I made after college were easy for me to both visualize and explain from the moment the ideas occurred. One result was that the process of making them became less interesting, since I knew in advance exactly what the outcome would be. Working alone in my basement studio lacked the community aspect of creating at school. Time spent sewing and quilting with my grandmother filled a void. Although my work was featured in a few New York exhibitions, my desire to continue making sculpture had declined significantly.[17]

~

One year after graduation, in May of 1996, I make the decision to devote myself exclusively to finding and documenting my grandmother's quilts. I am twenty-five; my grandmother is eighty. Over the summer I drive to New York, Maryland, Kentucky, and Pennsylvania to collect her quilts. Others are sent through the mail. Working with a professional photographer I begin the process of documenting close to two hundred quilts from seven different states.

~

I remember being amazed by the wide variety of patterns and the color combinations. One of Grandma's most unique quilts, made from hand-smocked panels, belongs to my mother (see figures 5 and 6). It reminds me of a summertime visit to Grandma's when I was about eight. I sat with my grandmother on the front porch glider and she taught me to hand-smock intricate designs on pleated fabric. Despite the humid summer air, we used red and green thread, and made Christmas ornaments by wrapping the fabric around styrofoam balls. For Easter decorations we used pastel-colored thread, and stitched the smocked material around styrofoam eggs. Even when I was in grade school, time spent with Grandma usually revolved around making things, from oil paintings to homemade pizzas.

Quilting lessons with my grandmother, as well as the memories that came to life while I collected and photographed her quilts, altered my perspective about this documentation project. It has not merely been about collecting, chronicling, and preserving works of art; it has been about being with Grandma and learning her story.

My grandmother, Mary (Yakimovicz) Sibley, was born on February 15th in 1916. Her parents were Veronica (Ciemierek) and George Yackimovicz; Mary was their seventh child. In later years the family would celebrate her birthday one day early, on the 14th of February. Grandma explained, "Mom always told me that I was her Valentine, even though I really wasn't." My great-grandparents, Veronica and George, went on to have six more children for a total of thirteen, including: Julia (who died as an infant), Matt, Blanche, Sally, Albert (Ab), Ann, Mary, Valentine (Valery, who

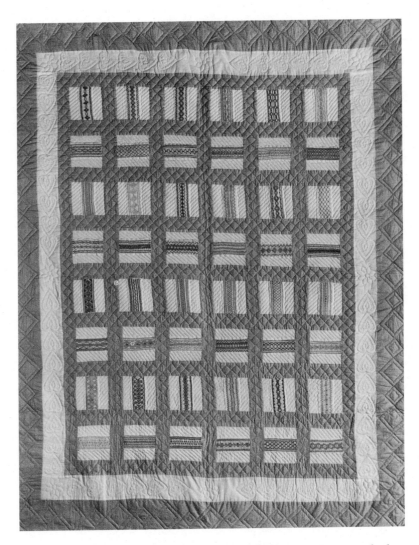

Figure 5. Smocked quilt, 88" x 99", circa 1985. Colors: white smocked fabric with multicolored needlework, surrounded by a pale blue print. Original design created entirely by Mary Sibley. Collection of Nancy (Sibley) Lenz. Photograph by Dennis Ryan.

Figure 6. Detail: smocked quilt, 88" x 99", circa 1985. Photograph by
Dennis Ryan.

also died as an infant), Joe, Frank, Gertrude (Nancy), Julia (Sadie),
and Florian (Jack or Ki).[18]

Veronica and George raised their large family in Arcadia, Pennsylvania. At the time it was a big mining town, "but those days
are long gone," my grandmother recently told me. Veronica and

Figure 7. Painted Poppies, 78" x 91". Circa 1984. Colors: red, orange, green, and white. Made by Mary Sibley for Jeannie (Sibley) Powell; collection of Peter and Gus Powell. Photograph by Dennis Ryan.

George were both immigrants from Poland; they met at a boarding house. George worked in the coal mines and Veronica ran her own business, a beer garden with a reputation for home-cooking on Saturdays.[19]

Although there was plenty of work to be done on the homestead, Veronica and George sent their children to school. In the home they spoke Polish so their children's education was deemed especially important, particularly learning to read and write in English. After attending a one-room school house, my grandmother graduated from a new high school. "If you can read a book you can do anything," she often tells me; the valuable lesson is also conveyed by virtue of her repeated example.[20] She has told me that when she wanted to learn to quilt she went to the library and checked out books on the subject.

My grandmother's mother, Veronica, was not a quilter. Her days were filled with the demands of raising her large family and running her business. While Veronica did not teach her daughters to quilt she did teach them to use the sewing machine. By the time my grandmother tried her hand at quiltmaking she was already a skilled seamstress. Equally beneficial for quiltmaking was the strong work ethic she inherited from her mother.

After graduating from high school and working for a few years in Philadelphia, my grandmother met and married Stephen Sibley. Her brother Jack told me that he remembers Steve courting her, and knocking on their door with chocolates in hand.[21] My grandparents decided to live in Gipsy, Pennsylvania, less than five miles from my grandmother's childhood home. Grandpa ran the town store with Grandma's assistance and together they raised four daughters, Katheryn (Katie or Kathy), Joan (Jeannie), Veronica, and Nancy, as well as a nephew, Whitney. When the children got older, they took in three foster daughters: Almeda, and sisters, Ruthie and Donna. Grandpa believed that the children in their home helped keep them young.

Grandma and Grandpa were both active in the church and the community. As a 4-H leader Grandma taught many of the neighborhood girls to sew. From the bountiful flowers in her gardens she made bouquets for the church.

When Grandma was fifty-eight, her husband had a sudden heart attack, and passed away. Grandma was too young to receive social security benefits and needed an income. She decided to take a job as a cook at the high school her foster daughters, Ruthie and Donna, attended. She worked until the age of sixty-five, the required retirement age at the time.

Afterwards, Grandma was finally free to spend her days as she pleased. In recent years she has told me, "I don't let the house rule me, I rule the house; the house ruled me for years" and, "The dishes can just wait, I've waited for them plenty of times."[22]

Over the years Grandma had several hobbies: gardening, landscape and portrait painting, and later bisque dollmaking. Grandma's interest gradually shifted away from dollmaking as the small brushes used to paint the doll's faces (down to their individual eyelashes) became more difficult for her to hold steady. Grandma's desire to make quilts grew, and just as oil painting was replaced by dollmaking, dollmaking would be replaced by quiltmaking. Grandma had learned to quilt about ten years before her retirement by participating in a few fundraising quilting bees at her church. After retiring she decided she would like to try quiltmaking on her own.

Around this time her city-dwelling daughter, Jeannie, became interested in collecting quilts and asked Grandma to keep her eyes open for potential bargains at garage sales and antique stores. According to Grandma, "That didn't last long because soon I was making the quilts she liked." Early examples include the Windmill created from white muslin and a taxicab-yellow cotton, and the appliqued, Painted Poppies (see figure 7). Grandma still has pattern books in which Jeannie drew a small "x" next to the quilts she wanted. She usually selected the fabrics of her choice as well. Jeannie appreciated the quilts her mother made and Grandma has told me, "She used to give me hell for not signing my quilts." Somehow, Jeannie did convince her mother to sew her signature on one quilt, featuring appliqued hearts and flowers. I asked Grandma about the lone signature, stitched in red, and she responded, "I told her she didn't need it, but she wanted it."[23]

When Grandma decided she wanted to quilt, she did not have a frame. This problem was temporarily alleviated by a neighbor who loaned her one. Grandma made a couple of quilts with the neighbor's frame, but soon it became apparent she would need one of her own. Not content to simply get a duplicate of one of the frames she had previously used, she visited the homes of other quilters to look at theirs. She made sketches of the ones she liked and took notes and measurements. She once told me, "Some of the frames I saw were so rickety I don't know how they were able to use them." When she was satisfied with the plans she had drawn, she consulted a local carpenter, Delbert Walker. He made the frame she desired, according to her specifications. Delbert would go on making and selling quilting frames based on her design. He later told her, "You really put me in business." Likewise, he helped put her "in business."[24]

Grandma has made a wide variety of quilts including: a navy blue and black copy of an Amish quilt (see figure 8), a scrap quilt made from brilliantly colored velvets with a diamond center (see figure 9), a Teabox (see figure 10), a Broken Star surrounded by peaks (see figure 11), and a scrap "quilt" made from upholstery fabric sewn into strips [it was too thick to quilt so she tied it instead] (see figure 12). She calls quilts made from scraps "freebies." She always saves her scraps, "Maybe there will be enough to make a baby quilt," she tells me.[25]

Grandma quilts the most when the weather is cold and wet: "I like to quilt on a rainy day, what else are you going to do when the weather's bad?" In the winter months, long days spent quilting are typical; in the summer she may take a brief hiatus to visit relatives. If a quilt is in progress she frequently continues working until the daylight hours wane. When we sew together and my mistakes increase in number at the end of the day, Grandma remains vital, encouraging me with, "I made a lot of mistakes when I was learning, I still do," or "You don't learn overnight, you learn by doing; I'm still learning." One evening I suggest stopping for the day when the machine becomes stuck, but Grandma responds, "Heather, I don't give up that easy."[26]

As a gift for my mother, we once put together a quilt of fifty-six plain white blocks with the main purpose of giving me something on which to practice quilting. Grandma told me:

> If you do half a block a day, that's one hundred and twelve days. Just try to do a little every day regardless of how much you do. I've seen women who take a whole year just to make one quilt. That's because they don't work on it every day.[27]

When piecing a quilt, Grandma has reminded me, "It goes faster when you do one thing at a time, I learned that. That way you can concentrate on one thing instead of half a dozen." While teaching me to quilt, she has advised me about my stitches, "If you continue

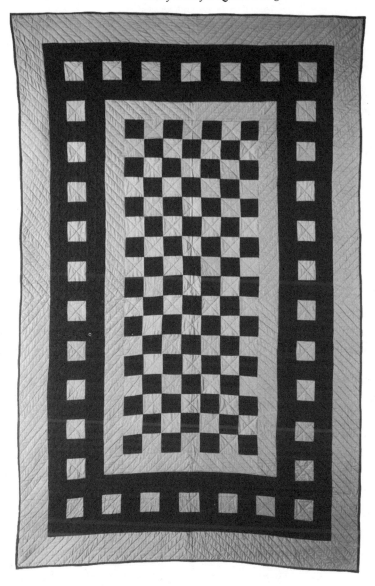

Figure 8. Copy of Amish quilt, 72" x 110", 1989. Colors: black and navy blue. Created by Mary Sibley for Gus Powell from his drawing of the original. This quilt is one of two matching quilts made for Gus' twin beds. Photograph by Dennis Ryan.

Figure 9. Velvet scrap quilt, 77" x 78", circa 1988. Colors: purple, green, red, black, and assorted prints in various colors. Made by Mary Sibley for Jeannie (Sibley) Powell from her fabric scraps. Collection of Peter and Gus Powell. Photograph by Dennis Ryan.

in that way you'll never get done. You need to pull the needle through in this way, making several stitches at once."[28]

Grandma has modestly commented, "I don't know why everyone likes my quilts so much." She focused on her grandchildren and continued:

The boys are as bad as the girls. David doesn't let the cats sleep on them. . . . Gus called me one midnight for advice on how to get a coffee stain out. . . . Lizzie doesn't want it if I didn't make it, but if I made it, she wants it.[29]

Figure 10. Teabox, 94" x 108", 1994. Colors: red, white, and three shades of blue. Made by Mary Sibley for Susan Mudry, friend of Kathryn (Sibley) Hill. Photograph by Dennis Ryan.

Recently, over the summer of 1997, Grandma made five quilts in three months. The recipients were typical: a daughter, a grandson, two granddaughters, and a friend. Money, as usual, was not exchanged. Although enough quilts have been made to cover all of her children, grandchildren, and great grandchildren, she pushes herself to continue until her elbow swells from overuse and her fingers are calloused from multiple pin pricks. Her doctor cautions

Figure 11. Broken Star, 94" x 104", 1983. Colors: pink, green, and white. Created by Mary Sibley for Elizabeth (Hill) Miller. Photograph by Dennis Ryan.

her to slow down, threatening to inject her elbow with cortisone to relieve the swelling.

Grandma Sibley's rigorous work ethic is paralleled by her abundant generosity. Only one of the quilts she has made remains in her home, and it is now well-worn. The recipients regard her quilts with a strong sentimental attachment, aware that labor has trans-

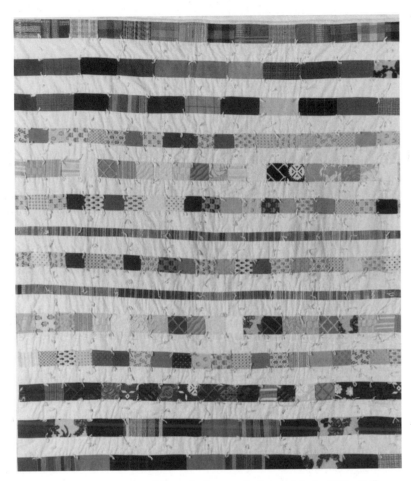

Figure 12. Scrap strip "quilt" made from upholstery fabric, 72" x 84", circa 1982. Colors: antique white, brown, green, blue, red, yellow, orange. Created by Mary Sibley. Collection of Kathryn (Sibley) Hill. Photograph by Dennis Ryan.

formed cloth and thread into a work of art intimately linked to its maker. My cousin Gus has told me that sometimes when he cannot sleep at night, he imagines Grandma making the tiny, little stitches in the quilt he sleeps beneath. He has likened the small, repeated hand gestures that she makes while quilting to the hand gestures he remembers her making in church while saying the rosary. "We would always get to church early so the ladies could do their rosaries before mass," he recalled:

> While waiting outside, Grandma, Rose, and the other women, would talk and sometimes gossip. The women had their rosary beads in their hands, wrapped around their wrists, or tucked into small secret pockets. I can remember standing alone behind my Grandmother's back and watching her slowly and conscientiously slide the string of brown beads out of her cupped hand, letting them leave her hand one at a time until they all hung quietly in the air. In the church I would kneel next to Grandma and focus on her hands, on her fingers that would hold each bead, the thumb that would move across them in a circular motion, and the quick movement that would take her from one bead to the next at the end of each prayer. As the group of women, never more than a dozen in number, would recite the prayers–rhythmically and in a high pitched, almost indecipherable cry–I would keep my attention on Grandma's hands. Her subtle finger movements became the ritual gesture of her prayers, the manual part of her good intentions.[30]

Another quilt recipient, Grandma's good friend Doris, was so happy when Grandma presented her with a quilt that she wept. Previously she had given Grandma some fabric "she wasn't going to get around to using." Grandma turned it into a Card Trick quilt and gave it to Doris, who was quite ill. A few days later she passed away. In spite of her sadness, Grandma commented, "I'm glad she had a little while to enjoy her quilt."[31]

Although Grandma's quiltmaking is a labor of love, the task fulfills another function. She credits her "hobby" with keeping her hands active and her mind alert. While she understates her accomplishments, my grandmother has told me, "My retirement years have been somewhat productive, maybe that's why I feel better than some of these old women who don't have anything to do but sit around and worry about themselves." At the age of eighty-one she commented, "I feel that I'm on borrowed time anyway. . . . my dad lived to be seventy-two and my mother lived to seventy-eight."[32]

Grandma lets few things disturb her. When a friend visits with her two young sons and they remove all the pins from her quilting frame, she laughs and responds, "That Parker, he's a live wire;" quickly adding, "Ian will always be my boy." Her response to losing a needle is, "I'll find it later, when I step on it." It frustrates her, however, to get a knot in the thread right at the beginning, or when she has to rethread her machine to sew one last inch, "That's what burns me up." She also dislikes making quilts in colors that do not go together, but, "If that's what they want. . ." Her own favorite color is blue. Finishing a quilt delights her, "I'm kind of tickled to see it done, it turned out better than I thought it would." Recently when an eighty-three-year-old woman moved into my grandmother's apartment building, she told me, "She's full of pep," so they must be two of a kind.[33]

Time spent with my grandmother has taught me about more than sewing and quilting. "Perseverance works," Grandma tells me while working on a quilt, and it is advice for life, not just quilt-making. I have also learned about cooking and gardening. My grandmother's green thumb is unmistakable. Besides using commercial fertilizers, such as Miracle Gro, she also makes use of natural fertilizers, such as banana peels. "Of course my plants grow," she comments, "I feed them." Likewise, she feeds anyone who is lucky enough to wander into her kitchen. She connects good nutrition to good health and believes in three fruits and four or five vegetables per day. But she also makes wonderful desserts. "I eat a little bit of everything," she has told me, "just like Julia Childs" and "I must be doing something right, I've lived this long."[34]

While learning to quilt my interest in contemporary art has remained and unexpected parallels have become obvious between my grandmother, working diligently at her quilting frame with repetitive gesture, and the techniques employed by established contemporary artists such as Ann Hamilton, Jackie Winsor, and Yvonne Rainer. Similarities have already been acknowledged between the appearance of traditional Amish quilts and the modern abstract paintings of Joseph Albers, Victor Vasarely, and Kenneth Noland.[35] The similarities that became apparent to me were more subtle, and concerned the process of making, specifically the use of repetitive labor among some of my favorite female artists.

Installation artist, Ann Hamilton, transforms everyday, nontraditional materials into works of art through repetitive gesture. For example, as part of her installation *Privation and Excesses*, she connected 750,000 pennies with honey.[36] Through an equally arduous process, sculptor Jackie Winsor makes pieces which are quite different than Hamilton's. In her sculpture *Fifty-Fifty*, Winsor used over 20,000 nails, all of which required predrilling holes and countersinking nail heads.[37] Yvonne Rainer, an experimental filmmaker trained as a dancer, used "tasks, repetition, and fragmentation in her work in order to isolate movement for its own sake, and to examine and value it as an entity in and of itself, calling attention to the beauty of ordinary, simple movements."[38]

Like Rainer, Hamilton acknowledges her interest in repetitive labor. She has stated, "I'm interested in the accretion of small gestures, in the way we build the world with them."[39] Typically, in Hamilton's installations "countless touches of individual hands permeate the piece."[40] As a result, her materials are embodied with "a residual accumulation of gestures," just like a quilt.[41]

Jackie Winsor is also aware of the importance of time and process in her work. She believes that sculptures "completed after considerable amounts of intense labor, are imbued with the same sense of age and experience that can be detected in an elderly human being." Winsor has stated, "When you look at someone who is 80 years old, you know they're made up of lots of days and weeks and months and years. . . . I relate that to the human being and I relate that to the pieces I make."[42] She has also commented on creating a specific sculpture, "Originally it wasn't my intention to put so many nails in the piece, but it seemed to take that much time to instill the piece with its own energy and presence . . . to seem complete."[43] Critic, Kirk Varnedoe, compares Winsor's work to a "mantra."[44] The point is especially pertinent; Winsor makes sculptures and my grandmother makes traditional quilts, but both experience positive meditative benefits from practicing their respective arts.

Besides allowing me to see connections between my grandmother's traditional quiltmaking and the aforementioned contemporary art, learning to quilt at my grandmother's side has been an amazing gift in itself. Philosopher, Lewis Hyde, believes that a gift has the power to bring "transformation."[45] In college I was taught that rigid boundaries necessarily separate "high" art from "low" art and that the former is superior to the latter. For me the boundaries have become less harsh. People who enjoy using their hands make things. Different people make different objects depending on their personalities and their environments. Some have learned to connect cloth with stitches, others have learned to apply paint to canvas. Paintings and quilts are both forms of personal expression as well as documents of time and place. Both are legitimate and both are important.

Quilting lessons have also enhanced my appreciation and understanding of gift labor. Watching Grandma give away the quilts on which she has labored so intensely, never ceases to impress me. Hyde has stated, "It is as if you give a part of your substance to your gift partner and then wait in silence until he gives you a part of his."[46] I am fortunate to have been exposed to my grandmother's wisdom, perseverance, generosity, strength, and love.

～

It is six o'clock A.M. in mid-November, 1997. My grandmother rises and turns on the kitchen light. She starts making coffee. The light and sound awaken me; I am sleeping on her living-room floor, visiting for a few days. She returns to her bedroom and listens to the morning news. Soon she will take her sewing machine from the closet and we will begin to sew. I am twenty-six. Grandma is eighty-one.

Acknowledgements

I would like to thank my parents, Nancy and John Lenz, for their unending support; everyone who lent quilts to be photographed; my cousin, Gus Powell, for his written statement; Katherine Blackbird, for her encouragement; and the Ohio Arts Council, for generously funding this documentary project.

 The Ohio Arts Council helped fund this project with state tax dollars to encourage economic growth, educational excellence and cultural enrichment for all Ohioans.

Notes and References

1. Mary Sibley, conversation with author while working on a quilt to-
    gether, recorded in my sketchbook, date not recorded, Clymer, PA. (I
    began documenting things that my grandmother said long before I con-
    ceived of this project in this format, sometimes I scribbled down her
    words on a cardboard quilt pattern or a scrap of nearby fabric. This pa-
    per is my way of passing her wisdom along.)
2. Ibid.
3. Ibid.
4. Robin Winters, "An Interview with Kiki Smith," in *Kiki Smith*, by Kiki
    Smith (The Hague: S.D.U. Publishers, 1990), 130.
5. Lynne Cooke, "The Viewer the Sitter and the Site: a Splintered Syn-
    tax," in *Ann Hamilton, tropos*, eds. Lynne Cooke and Karen Kelley (New
    York: Dia Center for the Arts, 1995), 71-73. Cooke stated, "For [Lewis]
    Hyde, labor is activity that is not generated primarily by the need for
    financial payment, and not calculated in hourly increments. It estab-
    lishes its own pace and hence is harder to quantify in terms of payment
    . . . it consequently belongs to an economy of exchange . . . and is cali-
    brated in terms of worth rather than value. Once wage earning and the
    accumulation of wealth became preeminent social goals, such types of
    activity are generally relegated to women. If the costs and rewards of
    gift labor lie outside market systems . . . the mercantile spirit necessarily
    suppresses the sympathetic faculty . . . marking and maintaining a dis-
    tinction between the self and others are the virtues of the mercantile
    spirit."
6. Lewis Hyde, *The Gift: Imagination and the Erotic Life of Property* (New
    York: Vintage Books, a division of Random House, 1983), 56. On the
    same page, Hyde continues, "I go into a hardware store, pay the man
    for a hacksaw blade and walk out. I may never see him again. The dis-
    connectedness is, in fact, a virtue of the commodity mode. We don't
    want to be bothered. If the clerk always wants to chat about the family,
    I'll shop elsewhere. I just want to buy a hacksaw blade."
7. Sibley, conversation with author.
8. Ibid.
9. Jeannie (Joan Sibley-Powell) studied fashion design at Moore College
    of Art and Design in Philadelphia, PA, and at the Sorbonne in Paris,
    France. After college, Jeannie started her own design business with a
    former classmate, *Sibley Coffee Ltd.* Later she worked for Ellen Tracy.
10. Sibley, conversation with author.
11. Ibid. Due in part to regional dialects, I found several different spelling
    for the following words: finger, fingers, and hand. When I asked Grand-
    ma Sibley about the Polish word she pronounced "pazooti" (Polish for
    fingers), she told me it was spelled *pazucy*.

12. Ibid.
13. Ibid.
14. Ricky Clark, "Sisters, Saints, and Sewing Societies: Quiltmaker's Communitites," in *Quilts in Communities: Ohio's Traditions, Nineteenth & Twentieth Century Quilts, Quiltmakers, and Traditions,* by Ricky Clark, George W. Knepper, and Ellice Ronsheim (Tennessee: Rutledge Hill Press, 1991), 131. Although the quilt discussed was not specifically intended as a mourning quilt, it is relevant to note Clark's statement, "The process of making a mourning quilt deeply involves the quiltmaker in a continuing relationship with the deceased." According to Clark, most mourning quilts "were made by mother's to commemorate the deaths of children." Clark also noted, "Often the quiltmaker uses fabrics that were intimately linked to the deceased."
15. Sibley, conversation with the author.
16. Ibid.
17. In 1996, Clare Bell, associate curator at the Guggenheim Museum, selected a piece I created to appear in the *11th Annual Small Works International* exhibition at the Amos Eno Gallery in New York, NY. The piece, a set of playing cards titled the *Interview Game,* is a spoof on the critic artist interview. After both decks have been shuffled, questions and answers (some of which have been lifted from contemporary arts magazines), are paired at random. For example:

Question: Were you interested in classical contrapposto and how it quivers on the threshold between hubris and some kind of real but repressed omnipotence?
Answer: I have begun to realize that the Neo-Impressionists were not altogether misguided when they flirted with science.

Interview Game has been sold at various galleries and museum stores including: the Los Angeles Museum of Art, the Guggenheim Museum, the Whitney Museum of American Art Store Next Door, and Printed Matter (in New York, NY).
18. Sibley, conversation with author.
19. Ibid., 3 November 1997.
20. Sibley, conversation with the author.
21. Jack Yakimovicz, conversation with the author, January 1998.
22. Sibley, conversation with author.
23. Ibid.
24. Ibid.
25. Ibid.
26. Ibid.
27. Ibid.
28. Ibid.
29. Ibid.

30. Augustus Powell, written statement (at author's request), Oberlin, OH, 1996.
31. Sibley, conversation with the author.
32. Ibid.
33. Ibid.
34. Ibid.
35. Robert Bishop and Elizabeth Safanda, *A Gallery of Amish Quilts: Design Diversity from a Plain People* (New York: E.P. Dutton, 1976), 7.
36. Sarah J. Rojers, "Ann Hamilton: details," in *the body and the object: Ann Hamilton 1984–1996,* by The Wexner Center for the Arts (Ohio: Wexner Center for the Arts, 1996), 8.
37. Dean Sobel, "Jackie Winsor's Sculpture: Mediation, Revelation, and Aesthetic Democracy," in *Jackie Winsor* by Dean Sobel with essays by Peter Schjeldahl and John Yau (Wisconsin: Milwaukee Art Museum, 1991), 33.
38. Cooke, 63. For more information about Yvonne Rainer's filmmaking, see Shelly Green, *Radical Juxtaposition: the Films of Yvonne Rainer* (New Jersey: The Scarecrow Press, Inc., 1994).
39. Dave Hickey, "In the Shelter of the Word: Ann Hamilton's tropos," in *Ann Hamilton, tropos,* eds. Lynne Cooke and Karen Kelly (New York: Dia Center for the Arts, 1995), 129.
40. Cooke, 75.
41. Rojers, 9.
42. Sobel, 26.
43. Ibid., 23.
44. Ibid., 31.
45. Hyde, 47.
46. Ibid., 15.

A Stitch in Crime:
Quilt Detective Novels

Judy Elsley

The author examined the surprisingly large number of detective novels that feature quilts or quilting. Although quilts and murder seem an unlikely match, there are remarkable similarities between quilts and detective novels; quilts work well as a focus for the genre. The theoretical points are illustrated with reference to detective novels in which quilts or quilters play a significant part. An annotated bibliography of nineteen quilt detective novels (and one play) is included.

Quilts and murder are like oil and water; surely they do not mix. Quilts, after all, represent everything that is comfortable and safe in a domestic setting while murder is the disruption of all that calm order. If we put those stereotypes aside, however, we find that much of the adult fiction featuring quilts, quilters, or quilting takes the form of mystery or detective novels.[1] A good place to start making such an assessment is Betty Reynolds's wonderful *Internet Quilt Fiction Bibliography*. Of the 63 books listed, 25 are detective or mystery novels, while 38 (which include short stories, plays and poetry), are not.[2] It seems, then, that almost half of the current quilt fiction available takes the form of detective novels.[3]

Before we get too carried away with what appears to be a unique pairing of detective novels and quilts, however, we need to realize how many detective novels focus on a particular interest. You like dogs? Try Susan Conant's *Gone to the Dogs* or *A New Leash on Death*.[4] Perhaps you prefer cats. Yes, there are sleuthing cats. Lilian Jackson Braun has written "The Cat Who" mysteries, including *The Cat*

Who Had 14 Tales and *The Cat Who Knew Shakespeare*.[5] Do you have an interest in twelfth-century England? Try the Brother Cadfael series by Peter Ellis. Closer to home, Tony Hillerman has written fourteen mysteries focused on Native American culture in the Southwest. If you enjoy cooking, you could try Diane Mott Davidson's *Catering to Nobody*, which the dust jacket describes as "a pretty tasty mystery . . . the recipes and loving descriptions of food are guaranteed to make your stomach growl."[6] Murder, it seems, mixes well with any hobby.

My aim, then, is not to show that mysteries about quilts are unique, because special interest mysteries are, in fact, common. Rather, I want to raise a few questions and attempt to answer them: what is the connection between quilts and murder, and why is the detective novel such a popular and successful genre for writing fiction about quilts? Although quilts and murder seem very different, there are some striking similarities that make the quilt detective novel such a popular form.

We need to begin by defining that term: "quilt detective novel." The most important characteristic is that quilts or quilters play a significant part in a murder mystery. In some cases, that means one particular quilt lies at the center of the solution to the crime as in Katherine Hall Page's *The Body in the Kelp*, Susan Glaspell's *A Jury of Her Peers*, Barbara Michaels's *Stitches in Time*, or Jill Paton Walsh's *A Piece of Justice*.[7] Often the main characters are quilters, as in Margaret Atwood's *Alias Grace* or Paula Gosling's *The Dead of Winter*.[8] Sometimes, the protagonist owns a quilt shop, as in Carolyn Banks's *Patchwork, a Novel of Suspense*, or Lizbie Brown's *Turkey Tracks*.[9] Or, the novel could be set in the context of a quilt show, as in Sara Hoskinson Frommer's *Buried in Quilts*, Jean Hagar's *Death on the Drunkard's Path*, or Aliske Webb's *Murder at the Quilt Show*.[10]

What makes a quilt such an adaptable feature of detective novels? For a start, a detective novel is constructed rather like a quilt. Both quilt and detective novel are composed of layers. In the case of a quilt, the top, batting, and backing fabrics constitute the layers; the whole sandwich held together with quilting stitches. The detective novel is also composed of layers, as literary critic Peter Huhn explained:

> The plot of the classical detective novel comprises two basically separate stories—the story of the *crime* (which consists of action) and the

story of the *investigation* (which is concerned with knowledge). In their narrative presentation, however, the two stories are intertwined. The *first story* (the crime) happened in the past and is–insofar as it is hidden–absent from the present; the *second story* (the investigation) happens in the present and consists of uncovering the first story.[11]

The detective novel comes to a successful close when the story of the crime and the story of the detective's uncovering of it coincide. The detective, in a sense, quilts the layers together to make one seamless story. For example, in Earlene Fowler's *Irish Chain*, the amateur sleuth and heroine of the novel, Benni Harper, solves the crime by making connections between a present-day double murder in a nursing home, and events that occurred forty years previously.[12] It is only when Benni takes an interest in the history of the Japanese internment during the Second World War that she is able to quilt together the two narratives that lead her to solving the crime. The detective's job and the reader's pleasure lie in the gradual stitching of the two narratives into a single, cohesive story. The novel ends, and a quilt is completed, when the layers, either textual or textile, are layered perfectly on top of one another.

But what of the batting, that vital third layer that gives weight and substance to the two outer layers? The personal lives and relationships of the characters in the detective novel comprise this layer. We are as interested in the detective's love life, his or her daily struggles, and the details of his or her life as we are in the solution to a crime. Writers understand how attached the reader becomes to a particular detective, often writing a series of novels featuring the same central character, as for example, Earlene Fowler's Benni Harper. When we first meet her in *Fool's Puzzle*, Benni is a young rancher, recently widowed, adjusting painfully to a new way of life and managing an art gallery.[13] By the second book, she has solved one murder, embarked on another, and met the visiting chief of police, Gabriel Ortiz. Sparks fly as the two spar with each other, both frustrated by and attracted to each other. In the third novel, Benni and Gabriel are married, and solving crimes together.[14] The reader cares as much about Benni and her tumultuous romance with Gabriel as about whodunnit.

Perhaps the most extreme example of how deeply we care about the daily fabric of the characters' lives can be found in Margaret Atwood's novel, *Alias Grace*. Atwood fictionalizes the historical case of Grace Marks, a young servant who was convicted of murdering her employer and his mistress in 1843. After spending many years in jail, Grace's conviction is revoked and she is released. This detective novel is unusual in that it is never clear whether Grace participated in the murder; and Atwood's novel, in which Grace tells her own story in painstaking detail, does not answer the question. Yet we care more about the daily texture of Grace's life than about her innocence or guilt, so that the resolution of the crime becomes almost irrelevant to the details of her life. Atwood's ability to evoke so vividly the consuming details of Grace's life make this a compelling novel. Usually, though, the reader moves towards the revelation of who-did-it; so a successful 467-page detective novel that never resolves the crime is a *tour de force* on the part of the writer. In the end, the skill and craft of the unseen hand of the writer or the quilter will determine the success of the particular text(ile).

The best fabricators, whether of quilts or detective fictions, work with the understanding that the reader or viewer comes with a set of very clear, if unstated, expectations. In a detective novel, we know there will be a murder, or two, within the first few chapters of the book. We expect to encounter several suspects, a lot of clues, some of which will be red herrings, and a gradual unfolding of events that will eventually reveal what actually happened, who committed the murder(s), and why. Just as there are specific rules about what constitutes a detective novel, most of us accept fairly clear rules about what makes a quilt. Most quilters know about using 100 percent cotton fabric, the virtue of tiny, regular quilting stitches, or the importance of balancing color and design. In its most traditional form, a quilt is as formulaic in structure and content as a detective novel. There is a pleasure in seeing a well-made, traditional quilt that is similar to the pleasure of reading a detective novel that fulfills all our expectations. As critic, Christine Anne Evans, said:

> Its [detective novel] wide appeal depends in large measure on its ease of access, and this easy access is premised primarily upon its reliance on familiar formal strategies. . . . They please because they show the reader what he or she already knows and wants to know again.[15]

That formula can be soothing and predictable, to the point that a friend of mine, an avid reader, describes detective novels as "Prozac in print."

Yet if a writer or quilter does no more than follow the rules, we end up with competent but uninspiring quilts, and rather dull detective novels. The pleasure lies not only in seeing the quilt or the novel done well, but also in seeing some variation on the pattern that tweaks traditional expectations, offering something new and different. Indeed, it is often the tension between keeping and breaking the rules that makes for an exciting quilt. For example, as a number of quilt historians have pointed out, many quilts made by rural Southerners, including African-Americans, went unrecognized as art until the last fifteen years because they broke the very rules I named above.[16] A single quilt might be made of a mixture of different textiles—polyesters, velvets, cottons, and silk—and the design may have an improvised look, as if the quilter started in one corner and worked inspirationally rather than mathematically. The quilt stitches, too, might take little account of size or tidiness. When we understand how the rules of quilting have limited our view of what makes an acceptable quilt, we can begin to recognize the brilliance of those rule-breaking quilts.

Quilts and detective novels, then, are simultaneously formulaic and flexible forms; on the one hand they conform to widely accepted conventions, while on the other, there is always room for creativity. That tension between keeping and breaking the rules, which makes both quilts and detective novels exciting, can be formulated as the distinction between what literary theorist Roland Barthes described as the "text of bliss" that disturbs our expectations, and "text of desire" which conforms to our expectations.[17] Most quilt detective novels can be categorized as texts of desire, living up to our usual expectations, but Atwood's novel, for example, acts as a text of bliss because by breaking the primary rule of the genre, that of resolving the crime, she invites us to rethink the predictable boundaries we had assumed.

The reader, then, begins a detective novel with the expectation of a murder and its resolution. But that murder represents a broader issue than that one particular crime. The murder often happens in a well-ordered, provincial world where such an event is both unexpected and shocking. The world to which we have been introduced is ruptured by the murder, shaking up the entire community. The fragile fabric of social relations is torn by the crime, and the successful detective, in revealing the murderer, helps the community to stitch itself back together. The community members cannot re-establish normal relations until the murder has been solved because they no longer know who is telling the truth, and who they can trust. As readers, we find this process of rupture followed by synthesis, comforting. We like to think we live in civilized, safe communities, and yet the nightly news and our own experience tell us that this is not always so. As Evans said, "detective fiction represents the symbolic reaffirmation of the civilized space, where evil in the form of murder represents the external source of the threat to it."[18]

A good example of rupture and reaffirmation of the civilized space can be found in Katherine Hall Page's novels featuring Faith Fairchild, a minister's wife, who is sufficiently affluent to spend her summers on Sanpere Island off the coast of Maine. Faith is a professional caterer, but spends much of her time caring for her small son, Ben, and plays an active part in the local community. This comfortable and safe world is shattered in *The Body in the Kelp* when a couple of murders take place. The entire island is implicated in the unexpected violence. We cannot return to catering and child care until the murderer is revealed and removed. As John Cawelti said, the classic detective novel "affirmed the basic principle that crime was strictly a matter of individual motivations and thus reaffirmed the validity of the existing social order."[19]

Quilts, like fictional detectives, offer us the safety, order, and tranquility of the world as we would like to know it. Evans used the word "consolatory" to describe detective novels, while many people describe quilts with a similar word: "comforter."[20] As Carol Chadwick said of Agatha Christie's plots, they are soothing:

> because of the basic underlying tenet of all standard murder mysteries. The reader always knows the mystery is going to be solved and good will triumph over evil. Unlike the tumult of the sixties, things in the world of the mystery are always orderly. The reader knows that all the riddles put forth in the beginning of an Agatha Christie mystery will be solved without ambiguity. [21]

Although there are exceptions, quilts appeal to us in large part because they suggest an orderliness and safety in a basically unsafe and chaotic world. The work of the Boise Peace Quilters illustrates this idea. Protesting against nuclear war, this group of Boise housewives and mothers have spent the last fifteen years making quilts to commemorate peacemakers across the globe. The quilt, as a symbol of order and comfort, works well for them; it counteracts the fact that we live in the dangerous world of nuclear proliferation.[22]

As well as providing comfort, both detective novelists and quilters make patterns. A good detective is the person who, unlike everyone else in the novel, is able to look at a collection of apparently haphazard data, and put it together in a cohesive pattern that leads to a true reading of the events. Quilters, too, are clearly makers of patterns. Most of the traditional quilt pattern names are derived from the everyday experience of the women who lived through often trying times. Drunkard's Path, Log Cabin, or Rocky Road to California suggest stories of hard times that women translated into quilt patterns that made the experiences bearable. Even today, many quilters use quilt patterns as a way to deal with difficult situations, as we can see in the many quilts that respond to Desert Storm.[23]

In Jill Paton Walsh's *A Piece of Justice*, Imogen Quy, an avid quilter and nurse at St. Agatha's College in Cambridge, shares this same passion for discerning patterns. At the beginning of the book, Imogen is looking at a quilt design with her quilt group, trying to distinguish the blocks so she can figure out the pattern. In many ways that initial scene acts as a synecdoche for the rest of the book as Imogen becomes increasingly involved in figuring out a mystery, and of course a couple of murders, connected with a famous mathematician. Her ability to dissect and understand the quilt pattern stands her in good stead to do something very similar with the lives and events of the people around her. Indeed, Imogen's facility in discerning patterns makes her such a good detective that she, not the local police, solves the mystery and reveals the murderer.

Like the detective novel, a quilt is usually shaped by specific borders that encompass the design, within which the pattern, however sophisticated, is worked out. Usually, the detective investigates a murder within an enclosed society of a limited number of relationships because the crime must be solved within the parameters of the world as it is presented to the reader. In the case of Imogen

Quy, she is bound by the limits of the small academic world of a Cambridge University. In Lizbie Brown's *Turkey Tracks*, Elizabeth Blair, an American widow living in Bath, England, finds herself enmeshed in the complicated relationships connected with the local stately home, Wetherburn. Jean Hager sets her novel, *Death on the Drunkard's Path*, in a bed-and-breakfast inn that hosts participants in a local quilting convention. There are as many ingenious ways to draw the perimeters of a social world as there are ways to enclose a quilt. For example, in Carolyn Banks's *Patchwork, a Novel of Suspense*, the protagonist, Rachel, has started a new life for herself in Austin, Texas, so her world is defined by the very few people she knows there. Paula Gosling isolates her characters, in *The Dead of Winter*, by placing them near the Canadian border in winter, and then deluging the small community with several snow storms.

Perhaps the most significant parallel between quilts and detective novels is the stress both place on an attention to detail. Quilting, the very symbol of domestic life, requires careful, detailed, patient work, while most crimes in detective novels are solved through an accurate reading of domestic details, whether the detective is male or female. We are all familiar with Sherlock Holmes's legendry ability to solve a crime by paying close attention to the details: Was the victim left or right handed? Did the dog bark at night? Why is the miser repainting his house?

For an illustration of the importance of details, we can look first at one of the earliest and then at one of the latest texts in the genre of quilt detective fiction. Susan Glaspell wrote *Trifles*, a one-act play, in 1916, and later translated it into the short story, *A Jury of Her Peers*. The local sheriff and the county attorney are called to a remote farm to discover who murdered John Wright, the owner, who has been strangled in his sleep. His wife is the chief suspect, but the men find no clues to convict her. While the men tramp around the farm looking for evidence, their wives, who accompany the two men, wait in the kitchen. They find a strangled canary in Minnie Wright's sewing basket, and when they look at her unfinished quilt project, they notice a change in the stitching:

> Here, this is the one she was working on, and look at the sewing! All the rest of it has been so nice and even. And look at this! It's all over the place! Why it looks as if she didn't know what she was about![24]

Putting the evidence together, the two women figure out that when John Wright killed her bird, the only lively and colorful thing in her house, Minnie murdered her husband out of loneliness and frustration. The central irony of the play is that the women, not the men, look carefully enough at the shabby kitchen to realize what happened and thus solve the crime. They decide to hide the evidence by restitching the quilt in order to protect Minnie Wright.

Margaret Atwood, in her novel, *Alias Grace*, published eighty years after Glaspell's play, makes domestic detail the ultimate focus of the book. In the story, Grace recounts her life with painstaking attention to the specific the jobs she did:

> The floor was dirty as a stable, and I wondered when it had last been given a good cleaning. I'd swept it first, of course, and now I was washing it in the proper way, kneeling down with each knee on an old clout because of the hardness of the stone, and with my shoes and stockings off, because to do a good job you have to get right down to it, and my sleeves rolled up past my elbows and my skirt and petticoats pulled back between my legs and tucked behind into the sash or my apron, which is what you do, Sir, to save your stockings and clothes, as anyone knows who has ever scrubbed a floor. I had a good bristle brush for the scrubbing and an old cloth to wipe up, and I was working from the far corner, moving backwards towards the door; for you don't want to scrub yourself into a corner, Sir, when doing a task like this. [25]

Grace tells these details as if she were being cross-examined in a trial, and in fact, she is—by Simon Jordan who is trying to establish if she is sane and/or guilty. While Atwood pays inordinate attention to domestic detail, at the same time she eludes the primary expectation of a detective novel by never solving the crime. Detail merely leads, in a thoroughly postmodern way, to more detail. The attention to detail has the effect of shifting the focus of the book from the sensational double murder to the routine minutiae of Grace's life. In effect, Atwood is suggesting that a woman's daily round is both more interesting and more important than murder, which is quite a radical reorientation of the usual cultural emphases we see in newspapers or television news reports.

Any good detective understands that details matter, even if he or she does not take them to Atwood's extreme. The genius of an exemplary detective is that he or she can pore through the deluge of domestic details to decipher the true meaning of the events. The detective has learned to read the clues, which to the reader appear to be written in an unknown language. The murderer, in effect, is the writer while the detective is the reader. In a parallel way, many quilts tell stories in a non-verbal language as women use their fabrics to inscribe what matters to them, as for example, women's suffrage at the turn of the century. Quilts have long been a way for women to express ideas, thoughts, and feelings, often in cipher, which they cannot or do not wish to commit to paper or speak out about. As Annette wrote as long ago as 1845 for *The Lowell Offering*:

> Yes, there is the PATCHWORK QUILT! Looking to the uninterested observer like a miscellaneous collection of odd bits and ends of calico, but to me it is a precious reliquary of past treasures; a storehouse of valuables, almost destitute of intrinsic worth; a herbarium of withered flowers; a bound volume of hieroglyphics, each of which is a key to some painful or pleasant remembrance, a symbol of—but, ah, I am poetizing and spiritualizing over my *patchwork quilt*.[26]

Such now famous quilts as Harriet Powers's Bible quilts are indeed "bound volume(s) of hieroglyphics" which we have learned to read in order to understand their true meaning.

As one might expect, when entering the traditionally woman-defined world of quilting, the detectives in quilt fiction are all female. Often, in fact, there is a male detective, the official arm of the law, with whom our heroine works or fights as she goes about solving the crime. In some novels, such as the Benni Harper stories, the heroine and the legal detective move towards romance and marriage, while in others, such as Jean Hager's *Death on the Drunkard's Path*, the surly Sergeant Butts is openly rude to Tess Darcy:

"Now, Miz Franks, get on with what happened," Butts said. "I'll decide if it was an accident or not. And I don't need any help from amateur snoops. I know how to do my job."[27]

Of course, we readers know that he does indeed need an amateur's help, and there are no prizes for guessing who solves the crime first.

The women detectives in these quilt novels prove in many ways different from their male counterparts. In "classic" detective novels, such as Conan Doyle's Sherlock Holmes stories, the detective remains at an emotional distance not only from the participants in the case, but from pretty much any other emotional entanglement. In the "hard-boiled" tradition of Raymond Chandler or Dashiell Hammett, the detective often becomes involved, but the attachment is dangerous or even fatal.[28] The amateur sleuths of detective fiction differ, too, from such female detectives as P. D. James's Cordelia Gray, or V. I. Warshawski's Sara Paretsky. Those tough loners operate in the hard, cold world of men, often drink, carry a gun, and can expect to be beaten up in the course of the book. The women detectives in most quilt novels have quite a different profile. For a start, they are amateur rather than professional detectives, often drawn into a crime because it happens in their community, not because they seek it out. Perhaps because of their amateur status, these women are almost never violent, and do not carry guns. In fact, they are usually stalwart members of their community rather than renegades or oddballs. For example, Elizabeth Blair, in Lizbie Brown's *Turkey Tracks*, is an American widow living in England, who has established herself in the community by opening a quilt shop. Jess Gibbons, in Paula Gosling's *The Dead of Winter*, is a single school teacher in her small Canadian community, and Tess Darcy, in Jean Hager's *Death on the Drunkard's Path*, also single, owns the local bed-and-breakfast house.

Apart from sharing a high level of independence, often out of necessity because they are single, divorced or widowed, these women detectives often form strong connections with other women. Faith Fairchild, in *The Body in the Kelp*, maintains a close friendship with the lively Pix; Imogen Quy, in *A Piece of Justice*, only becomes involved in solving murders because of her friendship with her lodger, Fran Bullion. Benni Harper is both helped and hindered by her energetic and curious grandmother, and the two wives in Susan Glaspell's *Trifles* establish a tentative friendship that leads to solving the crime.

Moreover, to a lesser or greater degree, these women are taking charge of their lives. In terms of the five stages of women's development, discussed in *Women's Ways of Knowing*, most of the protagonists have reached the fifth stage.[29] These five stages represent a movement from passivity to assertiveness, from no sense of self to self confidence. If we look at the earliest detective fiction, Glaspell's 1916 *Trifles*, we see the two women pass through the first two stages of "silence," where women view themselves as mindless and voiceless, and then "received knowledge," where women see themselves as capable only of receiving knowledge, not producing it. When the county attorney says, "No, Mrs. Peters doesn't need supervising. For that matter, a sheriff's wife is married to the law," he is presuming that his wife is no more than a receiver of knowledge.[30] By the end of the play, the two women probably have not passed beyond "subjective knowledge," a stage at which knowledge is conceived of as "personal, private and subjectively known or intuited."[31] That may well explain why they do not share the information about the true nature of the crime with the men.

Not surprisingly, most contemporary detective fiction shows women who have passed the fourth stage of development, that of "procedural knowledge" which is a "a position in which women are invested in learning and applying objective procedures for obtaining and communicating knowledge."[32] In fact, contemporary quilt detectives solve crimes *because* they have reached the fifth and final stage of development, that of "constructed knowledge," where a woman sees knowledge as contextual and experiences herself as a creator of knowledge. In effect, a detective can be defined as the person who generates the most plausible story to explain apparently mysterious events.

Finally, there is one more similarity: both quilts and detective novels find an academic home in a fairly recent area of study, "popular culture." In the past, many of my academic friends admitted their guilty delight in reading detective novels as if it were a sin to indulge oneself in such a way, and they certainly would not have included such books in their class syllabi. Yet such distinguished literary critics as Umberto Eco, Geoffrey Hartman, Frank Kermode, and Jacques Lacan have published essays on this particular genre, hopefully paving the way for more general acceptance.[33]

Quilts and detective fiction, then, go together like hand and glove: they are both simultaneously formulaic and flexible, thoroughly enjoyable, and often highly sellable. Moreoever, detective fiction provides a quilter with a convenient vehicle for writing, in great detail, about quilts and the business of making, showing, and selling them. Quilts and detective novels—it is a match made in heaven!

Acknowledgments

Publication of this paper has been generously supported by a gift from the Natalie Youngquist Memorial Fund of Ohio Valley Quilters Guild.

Notes and References

1. I will use the terms "detective novel" and "mystery" interchangeably in this paper, although technically the detective novel is a sub-genre of mystery novels.

2. Betty Reynolds, *Internet Quilt Fiction Bibliography*. http://www.nmt.edu/~breynold/quiltfiction.html.

3. A familiar quilt pattern often serves as the title to a quilt detective novel, indicating immediately the connection in the story between quilts and murder. For example, Lizbie Brown's *Broken Star* and *Turkey Tracks*; Earlene Fowler's *Fool's Puzzle*, *Irish Chain* and *Kansas Troubles*; and Jean Hager's *Death on the Drunkard's Path*. The particular pattern, however, does not necessarily play a part in the story.

4. Susan Conant, *Gone to the Dogs* (New York: Bantam Books, 1992); Susan Conant, *A New Leash on Death* (New York: Berkley Publishing Group, 1996).

5. Lilian Jackson Braun, *The Cat Who Had 14 Tales/The Cat Who Knew Shakespeare* (New York: Jove Books, 1992).

6. Diane Mott Davidson, *Catering to Nobody* (New York: Fawcett Crest, 1990).

7. Katherine Hall Page, *The Body in the Kelp* (New York: Avon Books, 1991); Susan Glaspell, *Trifles* (New York: Frank Shay, 1916), as reprinted in *Quilt Stories*, ed. Cecilia Macheski (Lexington: University of Kentucky Press, 1994), 194-206. [While all the other examples quoted in this paper are novels, *Trifles* takes the form of a play. In terms of content, however, it qualifies as a quilt murder mystery.]; Barbara Michaels, *Stitches in Time* (New York: Harper Collins, 1995); Jill Paton Walsh, *A Piece of Justice: An Imogen Quy Mystery* (New York: St Martin's Press, 1995).

8. Margaret Atwood, *Alias Grace* (London: Bloomsbury, 1996); Paula Gosling, *The Dead of Winter* (New York: Mysterious Books, 1996).

9. Carolyn Banks, *Patchwork: A Novel of Suspense* (New York: Crown Pub-

lishers, 1986); Lizbie Brown, *Turkey Tracks* (New York: Bantam Doubleday, 1995).

10. Sara Frommer Hoskinson, *Buried in Quilts* (St. Martin's Press, 1994); Jean Hager, *Death on the Drunkard's Path* (New York: Avon, 1996); Aliske Webb, *Murder at the Quilt Show* (Englewood, CO: Quilt Inn Publishing, 1995).

11. Peter Huhn, "The Detective as Reader: Narrativity and Reading Concepts in Detective Fiction," *Modern Fiction Studies* 33 (Autumn 1987): 452.

12. Earlene Fowler, *Irish Chain* (New York: Berkley Prime Crime, 1995).

13. Earlene Fowler, *Fool's Puzzle* (New York: Berkley Prime Crime, 1994).

14. Earlene Fowler, *Kansas Troubles* (New York: Berkley Prime Crime, 1996).

15. Christine Ann Evans, "On the Valuation of Detective Fiction: A Study in the Ethics of Consolation," *Journal of Popular Culture* 28 (Fall 1994): 160.

16. For a more detailed discussion of this issue, see: Cuesta Benberry, "White Perspectives of Blacks in Quilts and Related Media," in *Uncoverings 1983*, ed. Sally Garoutte (Mill Valley, CA; American Quilt Study Group, 1983), 59-74; Laurel Horton, "Nineteenth Century Middle Class Quilts in Macon County, North Carolina," in Ibid., 87-98; Gladys-Marie Fry, "Harriet Powers: Portrait of a Black Quilter," *Missing Pieces: Georgia Folk Art 1770-1976* (Atlanta: Georgia Council for the Arts and Humanities, 1976).

17. Evans, 160.

18. Ibid., 164.

19. John G. Cawelti, *Adventure, Mystery, and Romance: Formula Stories as Art and Popular Culture* (Chicago: University of Chicago Press, 1976), 105.

20. Evans, 159.

21. Carol S. Chadwick, "Nancy Drew—The Perfect Solution," in *Private Voices, Public Lives: Women Speak on the Literary Life* ed. Nancy Owen Nelson (Denton: University of North Texas Press, 1995), 47.

22. The Boise Peace Quilters was formed by women living in Boise, Idaho, in the early 1980s as a way to protest the proliferation of atomic weapons. This group of approximately forty women create sophisticated, one-of-a-kind quilts which honor individuals whose work encourages world peace.

23. See, for example, Nancy Cameron Armstrong, "Quilts of the Gulf War, Desert Storm—Participation or Protest?" in *Uncoverings 1993*, ed. Laurel Horton (San Francisco, CA: American Quilt Study Group, 1994), 9-44.

24. Glaspell, 201.

25. Atwood, 274.

26. Annette (pseudonym for Harriet Farley or Rebecca C. Thomson), "The Patchwork Quilt," *The Lowell Offering 5* (1845): 201-3; reprinted in *Quilt*

Stories, ed. Cecilia Macheski (Lexington: University of Kentucky Press, 1994), 11. (Page references are to reprint edition.)

27. Hager, 93.
28. Cawelti makes a useful distinction between the "classic" detective novel, and the later "hard boiled" detective novel. Briefly, the classic detective novel focuses on a single crime, an anomaly in an otherwise orderly and moral society. The detective does not indulge in romantic escapades, and always remains emotionally detached from the case and those involved. Sherlock Holmes would be a good example of the classic detective. The hard-boiled detective, however, often becomes entangled emotionally in the case, to the point that he is forced to make a moral choice at some point. The world of the hard-boiled detective is shot through with crime and sleaziness, the murder being merely the tip of the rotten social iceberg. Raymond Chandler's Philip Marlowe represents this second kind of detective. Most quilt detective novels are a hybrid: "classic" in that they usually assume an orderly world that has been temporarily disrupted by murder, but "hard-boiled" because of the degree of romantic and emotional attachments on the part of the protagonists.
29. Mary Field Belenky, Blythe McVicker Clinchy, Nancy Rule Goldberger, and Jill Mattuck Tarul, *Women's Ways of Knowing: The Development of Self, Voice, and Mind* (New York: Basic Books, 1986).
30. Glaspell, 206.
31. Belenky, 15.
32. Ibid.
33. Glenn Most and William W. Stowe have edited a useful collection of articles on detective fiction written by literary theorists and critics over the last two centuries. Many of them are seminal texts in the field. See Most and Stowe, *The Poetics of Murder: Detective Fiction and Literary Theory* (New York: Harcourt Brace, 1983) which includes: Jacques Lacan's "Seminar on *The Purloined Letter*," Umberto Eco's "Narrative Structures in Fleming," Frank Kermode's "Novel and Narrative," and Geoffrey H. Hartman, "Literature High and Low: The Case of the Mystery Story."

Annotated Bibliography of Quilt Detective Books

Atwood, Margaret. *Alias Grace.* London: Bloomsbury, 1996.
   A fictionalized account of an 1843 murder case in which Grace Marks was found guilty of murdering her employer, Kinnear, and his mistress, Nancy. Grace, who narrates most of the story, is a skilled needlewoman and quilter.
Banks, Carolyn. *Patchwork: A Novel of Suspense.* New York: Crown Publishers, 1986.

Rachel has started a new and anonymous life for herself in Austin, Texas, because she thinks her son, Drew, is a psychopath who wants to kill her. Someone, however, is still pursuing her. Rachel works in a quilt shop owned by Peyton, her only friend in Austin.

Brown, Lizbie. *Turkey Tracks.* New York: Bantam Doubleday, 1995.

Elizabeth Blair, a middle-aged American widow who moves to England, opens a quilt shop in Bath. She becomes involved in solving a murder committed at a local stately home, Wetherburn. Also by Lizbie Brown: *Broken Star.* New York: St. Martin's Press, 1993.

Dallas, Sandra. *The Persian Pickle Club.* New York: St. Martin's Press, 1995.

This story is about a group of Kansas women who quilt together, and protect one another from a dark secret.

Fowler, Earlene. *Irish Chain.* New York: Berkley Publishing Group, 1995.

Benni Harper, a widow in her thirties, is involved in a tumultuous romance with the new local police chief, Gabriel Ortiz. The two of them compete to solve a double murder at the local old people's home. Benni curates a local art museum that displays quilts.

Also by Earlene Fowler: *Fool's Puzzle.* New York: Berkley Prime Crime, 1994; *Kansas Troubles.* New York: Berkley Prime Crime, 1996; *Goose in the Pond.* New York: Berkley Prime Crime, 1997.

Frommer, Sara Hoskinson. *Buried in Quilts.* New York, St. Martin's Press, 1994.

Joan Spencer is the manager of the local orchestra, practicing for a recital at the prestigious annual quilt show. Joan becomes involved in solving the murder of the bossy show organizer, as well as helping to locate some missing quilts.

Glaspell, Susan. *Trifles,* first published New York: Frank Shay, 1916; reprinted in *Quilt Stories,* ed. Cecilia Macheski (Lexington: University of Kentucky Press, 1994), 194-206.

Originally published in 1916, this one-act play shows how two women solve a murder mystery by examining the log cabin quilt the suspect was piecing.

Gosling, Paula. *The Dead of Winter.* New York: Mysterious Press Books, 1996.

Jess Gibbons, a keen quilter, teaches home economics at the local high school in a small town near the Canadian border in Great Lakes country in the middle of a particularly cold winter. An ice fisherman discovers the body of a ne'er do well under the ice and Jess becomes involved in solving the mystery.

Hager, Jean. *Death on the Drunkard's Path.* New York: Avon, 1996.

Tess Darcy owns a bed and breakfast Victorian house, inherited from her aunt. She becomes involved in a quilting convention in town, as a number of her guests are participants. A famous quilter is killed at the convention, and Tess is drawn into the investigation.

Harper, Karen. *Dark Road Home.* New York: Signet, 1996.
Brooke, a defense attorney from Columbus, hides out from a stalker in Ohio Amish country where she temporarily manages a quilt shop employing local Amish women.

Lawrence, Margaret. *Hearts and Bones.* New York: Avon Books, 1996.
Midwife Hannah Trevor joins police officer Will Quaid to solve a murder in Maine in 1786. Hannah pieces together the evidence in the same way she pieces her quilts.

Mason, Sarah J. *Sew Easy to Kill.* New York: Berkeley Prime Crime, 1996.
Two detectives investigate the murder of a member of the community sewing class at St.Catherine's, a private girls' school.

Michaels, Barbara. *Stitches in Time.* New York: HarperCollins, 1995.
Rachel Grant works in a vintage clothing store where she encounters a mysterious antique album quilt that has magic sewn into it.

Page, Katherine Hall. *The Body in the Kelp.* New York: Avon Books, 1991.
Faith Fairchild is renting a cottage on Sanpere Island, off the coast of Maine, when Matilda Prescott, a wealthy widow, dies leaving a quilt top inscribed with the words "Seek and ye shall find." The quilt, which is sketched at the beginning of the book, becomes a map for finding hidden treasure and a clue in solving a couple of murders. Also by Katherine Hall Page: *The Body in the Basement.* New York: St. Martin's Press, 1994.

Paton Walsh, Jill. *A Piece of Justice: An Imogen Quy Mystery.* New York: St Martin's Press, 1995.
Imogen Quy, an avid quilter and nurse at St. Agatha's College in Cambridge, becomes involved with a mysterious biographical project taken on by one of her lodgers, Fran Bullion. The key to the mystery, and several murders, lies in a particular quilt owned by farmers in Wales.

Sutton, Margaret. *Clue in the Patchwork Quilt.* New York: Grossett & Dunlap, 1941.
In this novel for young adults, detective Judy Bolton solves the mystery of her missing cousin through a patchwork memory quilt. The author's heirloom bowtie quilt served as the inspiration for this book.

Taylor, Phoebe Atwood. *The Crimson Patch; an Asey Mayo Mystery.* New York: W.W. Norton, 1936; reprint Woodstock, VT: Foul Play Press, 1986.
Originally published in 1936, and set in rural Cape Cod, this story features a murder victim found wrapped in a quilt.

Webb, Aliske. *Murder at the Quilt Show.* Englewood, CO: Quilt Inn Publishing, 1995.
A murder mystery set at a local quilt show.

Stitches in Time:
The Development of Sewing Thread
in the Nineteenth Century and Beyond

Jenny Yearous

One of the most overlooked, yet potentially important, aspects of any sewn item is the thread with which it is sewn. The number of plies, the construction method, and the materials used all point to when a type of thread was made. Sewing thread has undergone many changes through time as a result of technological advances, including the invention of the sewing machine, mercerization of cotton, and the introduction of synthetic fibers. While documentation for these changes is often sketchy, there are means by which the changes can be traced, including examination of thread in extant and dated textiles and analysis of advertisements for sewing thread. Consequently, changes in manufactured sewing thread can provide clues to the manufacture date for sewn textiles such as quilts.

> All around the cobbler's bench
> The monkey chased the weasel
> The monkey thought t'was all in fun
> Pop goes the weasel
> A nickel for a spool of thread,
> A penny for a needle
> That's the way the money goes,
> Pop goes the weasel.
> English folk song[1]

Sewing thread can prove to be an important tool in determining the possible age of a textile such as a quilt. In the fall of 1996 and the winter of 1997, I was fortunate to be able to study fifteen quilts from the private collections of Sara Dillow and Mary Ghormley.

These quilts were featured in an exhibit of nineteenth-century quilts held in the gallery at the University of Nebraska-Lincoln, Department of Textiles Clothing and Design, in March of 1997. Under the direction of Dr. Patricia Crews, I analyzed the quilts with the hope of better understanding the fabrics and thread. The ultimate goal of that project was to determine the possible manufacture dates of the quilts and to confirm the dates the owners already had for them.

Barbara Brackman's book, *Clues in the Calico*, became a very important source of information to help date the quilts, especially her discussion of Grace Rogers Cooper's research on the changes in thread through time.[2] Cooper had indicated some very clear-cut dates for the introduction of certain types of thread. She suggested that 3-ply manufactured thread was introduced around 1800, 6-ply thread around 1840, and 6-cord thread around 1860.[3]

One of the quilts in the exhibit, a Baltimore Album quilt owned by Sara Dillow, held confusing clues to its probable date of manufacture. Baltimore Album quilts like this one were usually made between 1845 and 1855, a few years before 6-cord thread was supposedly available.[4] This quilt, however, contained 6-cord thread. While it is possible that it was sewn and quilted in the 1860s after the Baltimore fad had faded, another possibility was that 6-cord thread was available earlier than previously thought. Thus I began the research on when manufactured sewing thread came into existence, what changes thread went through during the nineteenth century, and when the changes occurred.

To use thread as a dating tool, one must obtain a sample of thread large enough that it can be untwisted to find the number of plies that make it up. It is the number of plies and how those plies are twisted together that determine a thread type. It is not always possible to obtain a thread sample from the sewing and the quilting threads for use in the analysis of a quilt without damaging the quilt, but when thread can be obtained, it proves to be a useful tool. Knowing when a new thread type was introduced helps to determine the earliest date an item may have been made.

Thread is made up of a series of plies or cords twisted together. Twisting and plying of strands of fiber create a stronger unit than the original strands. A ply is made up of two or more strands twisted together while a cord is made up of two or more plies twisted together. As mentioned, the earliest manufactured thread was 3-ply, which consisted of three single strands twisted together (see figure 1). Two-ply thread has two strands, 4-ply has four strands, 6-ply has six strands and so on. On the other hand, a 6-cord thread consists of three plies with each ply made up of two strands each. Four-cord would only use two 2-ply threads to make the finished thread (see figure 1).

Events Leading to the Invention
of the Manufactured Cotton Thread

Today we take for granted going to the store and buying a spool of thread. This has not always been the case. It was not until about 1800 that manufactured cotton thread was available to the hand sewers of the United States and Europe and only after 1820 that thread came on a wooden spool.[5] Before 1800, textiles were sewn with silk or linen thread and, rarely, homespun cotton or wool thread.

In the mid-eighteenth century the Industrial Revolution began. The textile manufacturing processes were some of the first to change, including the changes that resulted in the manufacture of cotton sewing thread.

James Hargreaves, in 1764, invented the spinning jenny, which greatly increased the speed at which yarn could be spun. Hargreaves's invention was not appreciated in its time; story has it that his machines were destroyed by a mob of handspinners who were afraid of losing their livelihood.[6] The yarns made on a Hargreaves spinning jenny only had enough twist to make them sufficiently strong for use as weft yarns in woven goods. They were not suitable for the warp yarns in weaving or for sewing thread.

In 1769 Richard Arkwright designed a water-spinning frame that, unlike the spinning jenny, had a continuous operation from carding to spinning. Ten years later Samuel Crompton, in 1779, combined aspects of both Hargreaves's and Arkwright's inventions into the spinning mule. With either Arkwright's or Crompton's inventions, cotton could now be spun into a fine smooth cotton yarn suitable for either warp or weft yarns but they were still not suitable for sewing thread.

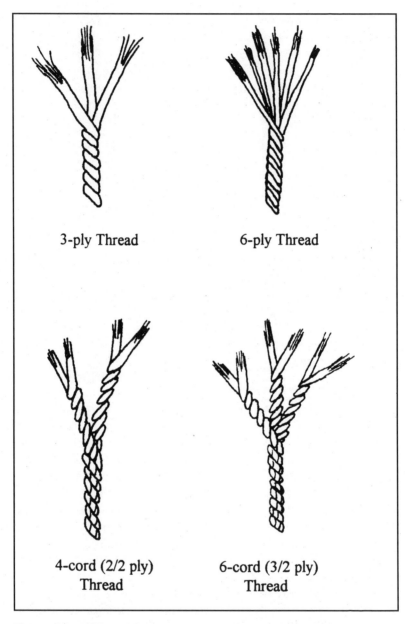

3-ply Thread   6-ply Thread

4-cord (2/2 ply)   6-cord (3/2 ply)
Thread   Thread

Figure 1. Drawings of the construction of the most commonly encountered thread types. Drawings by the author.

Plans for Arkwright's water-spinning frame made their way to the United States, despite England's attempt to prevent exportation of the plans or the emigration of those who knew how to build and operate the equipment. Samuel Slater, after an apprenticeship with Jedediah Strutt, a partner of Arkwright, immigrated to the United States and was soon hired to run the Arkwright-like frames owned by William Almy and Moses Brown, businessmen of Pawtucket, Rhode Island. Slater quickly made improvements in their equipment, making the business the first successful cotton textile concern in the United States. The yarns spun on this early equipment were suitable for weaving but were still not strong enough for hand sewing.[7]

The Invention and Early Development of Manufactured Cotton Sewing Thread

Cotton sewing thread was first manufactured in either the late 1790s or early 1800s; the exact date remains uncertain. There were two independent inventions of manufactured cotton thread around this time, one in the United States, the other in Scotland.

Tradition attributes the United States invention to Hannah Wilkinson Slater, the wife of Rhode Island textile manufacturer Samuel Slater.[8] According to the story, one day in 1793 or 1794, Mrs. Slater was at Slater's mill in Pawtucket and admired the smooth even yarns that were being spun there for weaving. She took some yarns home and spun them together on her spinning wheel into a plied thread suitable for sewing. Thus she created the first no. 20, 2-ply thread.[9] To test the quality of her thread, she sewed a sheet halfway with linen thread and finished with cotton thread. Supposedly the cotton thread outlasted the linen. While this account of the U. S. invention of cotton sewing thread is believable and even shows up in accounts as early as 1831, there will always remain some doubt as to its authenticity.[10]

George S. White, Slater's biographer stated that Slater immediately began, in 1794, the manufacture of cotton thread in his textile mills.[11] Other say it was not until a few years later, in 1797, that the first thread was manufactured.[12] By 1809, William Almy and Moses Brown, one-time partners of Slater, were making and selling cotton sewing thread. A Boston newspaper advertisement stated that the Factory Cotton and Thread Store had "five hundred pounds Cotton THREAD, in hanks, from No. 12 to 60, of superior quality and very white" for sale.[13] An 1810 advertisement from Hartford, Connecticut, shows that Almy and Brown made yarn, cotton twist, weavers' filling, sewing thread, and cloth of varying kinds.[14] Sewing thread, sold as hanks at this time, was a side product of some spinning mills. It was not until later that thread became commonly produced at mills dedicated to its manufacture. For example, the textile mills begun by Michael Schenck, in 1813, near Lincolnton, North Carolina, eventually developed the Lily brand sewing threads.[15]

In Europe the invention of manufactured cotton thread is attributed to Patrick or Peter Clark in the early 1800s. Most sources attribute it to Patrick Clark, while George A. Clark, sole agent in America for Clark's O.N.T. spool cotton in the 1880s, attributed it to Peter Clark.[16] It is possible that Patrick and Peter are the same person but no evidence of that has yet been found. Patrick and his brother James made silk heddle twine in Paisley, Scotland, for the local weaving mills. Heddle threads were made of silk until 1806 when the French trade with England was cut off by Napoleon. Consequently, silk was no longer available in England to make the silk heddle threads. The Clarks turned to cotton as a possible alternative to silk. The smooth cotton thread proved to be an excellent substitute for silk and remained in use even after silk was again available. The Clark brothers quickly saw the potential use of these heddle threads as sewing thread. This new cotton heddle twine was smoother and more even than the linen sewing thread commonly in use at this time.

During the first half of the nineteenth century, most thread sold in the United States was from European manufacturers.[17] Edward Bains stated that 1,187,601 lbs. of thread were sent abroad from England in 1833.[18] While he does not indicate who imported the thread, some of it had to be reaching the American market.

James and Patrick Clark, the men attributed with the invention of manufactured sewing thread, built their first thread factory in Paisley, Scotland, in 1812. James Clark's sons, James Jr. and John, took over the business, forming J. & J. Clark Co. They were the first to put thread on a wooden spool around 1820.[19] The Clarks handwound each spool with 3-ply cotton thread and charged the customer a half penny deposit on the spool, which would be refunded when the customer returned the spool. In 1864, George Aitkin Clark and William Clark, grandsons of James Clark, opened a cotton thread mill in New Jersey. [20]

James Coats, another predominant manufacturer of sewing thread began producing thread in Ferguslie, Scotland, around 1815.[21] James Coats's sons, James and Peter, formed J & P Coats Company. Harry Ballam and Coats and Clark publications suggest that both Coats threads and Clarks threads were introduced to the United States around 1818 or 1820.[22] Grace Cooper suggested that it was not until 1840, when Andrew Coats, brother to James and Peter Coats, became the first selling agent for J & P Coats in the United States, that Coats thread first became available to American markets.[23] Regardless, by 1869 the Coats began to manufacture sewing thread in Pawtucket, Rhode Island.[24] In 1896, J & P Coats merged with J & J Clark, but each continued to produce thread under their own names.[25]

Homespun Cotton Thread

In studying the changes in manufactured cotton thread, it is important not to forget the importance of its homespun beginning. A great deal of information is gleaned from studying homespun thread and its implications in the dating of quilts and other textiles.

The earliest cotton sewing thread was homespun. It is likely, especially in the cotton-producing states, that some late-eighteenth and early-nineteenth-century textiles were sewn with homespun cotton thread, probably 2-ply. I have seen one quilt, dating from the very late-eighteenth to early-nineteenth century, sewn with irregular 2-ply cotton thread that appeared to be homespun.[26] Barbara Brackman, a noted quilt researcher and author, described a quilt, dated 1798, sewn with what appears to be homespun cotton thread.[27] The maker was from Virginia and would have had access to cotton. Cooper described some Copp family textiles, most of which date to the latter part of the eighteenth century and one which dates to the first quarter of the nineteenth century, as having 2-ply cotton threads. Other Copp textiles were sewn with combinations of 3-ply cotton thread, 2-ply cotton thread, and 2-ply linen thread.[28] The availability of manufactured cotton thread did not immediately cause the abandonment of linen or other homemade threads. It also cannot be assumed that with each new improvement all the old thread was thrown out and the new thread was used exclusively.

It must be pointed out that homespun cotton thread is not always an indicator that it was made in a Southern state where cotton was grown. Manufactured warp and filling cotton yarns could be handplied into sewing threads much like Hannah Slater's first cotton thread. In a spirit of economy, thrums, weavers' threads left on the loom after the fabric is cut off, could be spun into sewing thread too.[29] Almy and Brown of Rhode Island sold warp and filling cotton yarn to markets as far away as New Hampshire.[30] Thus machine-spun yarns were available to spinners throughout the New England states for making into homeplied thread if they chose to make their own cotton thread.

While it seems likely that 3-ply cotton threads are machine-made rather than handspun, it cannot necessarily be inferred that 2-ply is an indication of homespun or homeplied thread. Edward Bains suggested that 2-ply, 3-ply, and 4-ply threads were machine-made in the 1830s in Manchester, England, and in Scotland.[31]

Finally, we cannot assume that all homespun 2-ply threads date only to the eighteenth or early nineteenth centuries. In the South during the Civil War, many women were forced by necessity to spin their own thread for weaving and sewing. Parthenia Hague, a young schoolteacher living on an Alabama plantation during the Civil War, wrote of her wartime experiences. She told how they made-do, to compensate for the many manufactured goods they could no longer buy from the industrial North:

> Our sewing-thread was of our own make. Spools of "Coats'" thread, which was universally used in the South before the war, had long been forgotten. For very fine sewing-thread great care had to be used in drawing the strand of cotton evenly, as well as finely. . . . From broaches of such spun sewing-thread balls of the cotton were wound from two to three strands double, according as coarse or fine thread was needed.[32]

Changes to Manufactured Cotton Thread

At first, the most common cotton thread commercially available to handsewers was 3-ply, though 2-ply and 4-ply were also available.[33] Around 1840 cotton thread went through a change to 6-ply (see figure 1). This 6-ply thread did not gain popularity and was not widely sold.[34] When Grace Cooper served as curator of the Division of Textiles, National Museum of American History, Smithsonian Institution, she analyzed more than thirty early American flags dating from ca. 1800 to ca. 1870 and found only seven contained some 6-ply thread.[35] Other threads found in Cooper's study were 2-ply and 3-ply linen, 2-, 3-, 4-, and 5-ply cotton, and 2/2-ply (4-cord?) and 3/2-ply (6-cord) cotton threads.

Changes in sewing thread seem to be directly tied to the development of the sewing machine in the 1840s and 1850s.[36] At the time of the widespread distribution of the sewing machine, in the 1850s, the most common thread options were 3-ply or 6-ply cotton thread, silk thread, or linen thread. All of these proved to be inadequate in some way. The 3-ply cotton thread had a glaze finish and was too wiry and uneven for use in sewing machines and 6-ply cotton thread was too thick.[37] Regular silk and linen threads were either too weak or too thick to use in a sewing machine. Early sewing machines required a high quality thread that combined strength and fineness. A 3-ply silk thread, known as machine twist, was available by 1852. It combined strength with fineness, but was too expensive for most people.[38] Improving cotton thread seemed the only option for an inexpensive alternative to silk machine twist. Since two to four times more thread is needed to sew an item by machine than by hand, an improved cotton thread could prove profitable to its producers.[39]

Around 1850 cotton thread went through another metamorphosis into what is known as 6-cord thread, which consists of three plies of two single strands each (see figure 1). According to current industry conventions, 6-cord thread would be designated a three, 2-ply cord. George Aitkin Clark is attributed with perfecting 6-cord thread during the early 1860s for use in sewing machines.[40] He introduced it to the market as O. N. T. or Our New Thread. Clark's 6-cord thread proved to be the best thread for a sewing machine, combining fineness with strength, and it was inexpensive. In 1880,

George A. Clark, the sole agent in the United States for Clark's
O. N. T. wrote:

> In fact, the sewing machine came into a world with no thread ready
> for it, thirty years ago [1850]. It called for a mathematical roundness
> and precision of size, strength and tension, and a smoothness of finish,
> such as had never before been thought of in thread. . . . By reduplicat-
> ing many times over the refining processes at their command for the
> staple, the yarn and the cord; by the introduction of still finer machin-
> ery for carding, combing, and drawing the cotton; by substituting yarn
> finer by half in every number of thread, and doubling the number of
> yarns in the twisted product; by these and other novel refinements the
> modern six-cord spool cotton was soon perfected as the "true yoke-
> fellow" of the sewing machine.[41]

Other manufacturers adopted Clark's construction for their thread,
quickly making 6-cord thread the industry standard.

George A. Clark indicated that 6-cord thread was already being
made when George Aitkin Clark came to the United States in 1855
and that he only improved it by making it suitable for use with the
sewing machine.[42] I originally thought that Clark was referring to
the 6-ply thread that had been manufactured since about 1840, but
a *Scientific American* article dated 1850 states that C. E. Bennett of
Portsmouth, New Hampshire, received a gold medal in 1850 at the
fair of the American Institute for manufacturing "superior six-cord
Spool Cotton."[43] While we may never know whether Bennett's
thread had 6-ply or a 6-cord construction, this article is the first to
use the term 6-cord to designate the construction of thread.

Recent analysis of twenty-four quilts with inscribed dates ranging from 1841 to 1859 found nine quilts which contained 6-cord
thread.[44] Each of the nine quilts found to contain 6-cord thread
had it used as either sewing or quilting thread (see table 1). This
suggests that Bennett's thread could have been a true 6-cord thread
as the *Scientific American* article indicated.[45] This also implies that
the date of the introduction of 6-cord thread may not be as late or
clear-cut as Cooper made it seem.[46] Analysis of these date-inscribed
quilts and further research shows that 6-cord thread was possibly
available for use around 1850. While it is possible that a quilt could
be quilted after the blocks were made, the top assembled, and the
date inscribed by ink or embroidery, it seems unlikely that all of

Table 1. Results from the analysis of the thread found in date-inscribed quilts made prior to 1860 found in the Ardis and Robert James Collection in the International Quilt Study Center at the University of Nebraska-Lincoln.

Accession Number	Date	Thread	Uses
1997.007.935	1821	3-ply	quilting
1997.007.749	1838	3-ply	quilting
1997.007.876	1841	6-cord	quilting
1997.007.421	1842	6-ply	quilting
1997.007.458	1842	6-ply	quilting
1997.007.697	1843	6-cord	quilting
1997.007.479	1844	4-cord	quilting
1997.007.955	1844	3-ply	basting
1997.007.444	1846	6-ply	quilting
1997.007.520	1847	6-ply	quilting
1997.007.023	1851	6-cord	quilting
1997.007.666	1851	6-cord	quilting
1997.007.149	1852	6-cord	quilting
1997.007.780	1852	6-ply	quilting
1997.007.570	1853	6-cord	sewing and quilting
1997.007.665	1853	4-cord	quilting
1997.007.832	1853	6-ply	quilting
1997.007.869	1853	3-ply	quilting
1997.007.654	1854	4-cord	sewing
1997.007.774	1854	6-cord	quilting
1997.007.908	1857	3-ply	quilting
1997.007.720	1858	3-ply	quilting
1997.007.730	1858	6-cord	quilting
1997.007.859	1859	6-cord and 4-cord	quilting

Note: All threads analyzed were cotton machine-made thread. Sewing thread could not be analyzed in all cases because it would have meant damaging the quilt to obtain a sample large enough to untwist. In the cases where sewing thread was available for analysis either it was only a quilt top or it was a damaged quilt where sewing threads were available without further damaging the quilt.

these quilts can be explained by this theory. One quilt had the date of 1852 quilted in with 6-cord thread.[47] The quilts made prior to 1850 that contained 6-cord thread were probably quilted some time after being dated with ink. Until other quilts or dated textiles of a similar age are found containing 6-cord thread, the date for the introduction of 6-cord thread cannot be taken back further than 1850s.

Little is written about the 4-cord thread similar to that noted in a number of quilts from the James Collection. Consequently I can, at present, only guess as to its origins. Edward Bains indicated that 2-ply, 3-ply and 4-ply threads were being manufactured in Manchester, England, and in Scotland in the 1830s. One can only suppose that some of the 4-ply thread made at this time actually had a corded construction thus making it, in reality, a 4-cord thread. Cooper described a flag, dating to the first quarter of the nineteenth century, as having "2/2 cotton" thread in it. This designation suggests that the thread has 4-cord construction since other flags are described as having "4-ply thread."[48]

While I found only limited examples of 4-cord thread, it seems to appear in use early in the nineteenth century and it shows up periodically in quilts and other textiles well into the twentieth century. There are at least seven quilts ranging in date from 1844 to 1912 in the James Quilt Collection at the University of Nebraska-Lincoln that contain 4-cord thread, which is of two, 2-ply construction.[49] The most recent indication of 4-cord thread is found in the Fall/Winter 1960-1961 Sears catalog, which advertised 4-cord quilting thread.[50] Further research needs to be done in order to find when 4-cord thread was introduced and when it was made in order for it to become a useful tool in dating quilts and other textiles.

Changes to Sewing Thread in the Twentieth Century

Little is written about the changes that manufactured cotton sewing thread underwent over time. Changes in sewing thread did not stop with the invention of 6-cord cotton sewing thread; developments have continued through the years. Since there is so little published, I sought other sources of information that would lead to a better understanding of these changes in sewing thread.

Advertisements document some of these changes in their images and descriptions of the products. Advertising trade cards were a means for manufacturers to get their product name before the public. The earliest advertising cards date to around 1810, but they did not reach their height of popularity until 1880 to 1900.[51] Advertising cards had colorful pictures on them, often of the product in use, others with just a general scene.[52] One of the earliest known thread advertising cards is one for Clark's O.N.T. from 1872.[53]

Thread advertising cards often have pictures of the spool ends. Consequently, the trade cards seemed to be an excellent source for how spools looked from the 1870s to the 1900s. I expected to find that changes in the end labels could be charted based on these cards, but I observed no changes to the spool ends illustrated on these cards. The spool ends from 1880 to 1900 look the same as spools from the first quarter of this century.

The spool ends shown in the advertisements for Clark's O.N.T. usually show the bottom label which does not indicate the type of thread; it is the top label that clearly states that it holds "Clark's Best Six Cord" (see figure 2). The trade cards for Merrick Thread Co., Kerr & Co., and J & P Coats all show spool ends that clearly state that the thread is also 6-cord (see figure 3). While a card for Willimantic Thread does not show a spool end, the card does state that the thread is 6-cord spool cotton. These advertising cards clearly show that 6-cord thread remained the industry standard in the latter part of the nineteenth century and the early-twentieth century.

I also decided to examine changes in thread as reflected in the entries in the Sears, Roebuck and Company (Sears) catalogs, by checking the sewing threads offered for sale in both the Spring/Summer and the Fall/Winter catalogs between 1895 and 1972. The Sears catalogs provided a glimpse of the changes and developments in machine-made thread in the late-nineteenth and twentieth centuries. While Sears did not necessarily offer products when they first came on the market, the Sears catalog was often the first time some consumers saw or had access to a product. Therefore, products listed in the catalogs represent items commonly available to the general public throughout the twentieth century.

The first Sears catalog was published in 1891 and was devoted to watches.[54] By 1893 the catalogs were advertising a variety of items, including sewing machines; however, it was not until 1896

that sewing thread was first sold by Sears. In 1896 Sears offered
6-cord cotton thread as well as silk and spool linen threads for
sale.[55] Sears ceased its sale of thread in the catalogs in the 1970s, so
changes in sewing threads could no longer be monitored through
this source.[56]

In 1905, 3-cord thread began to be advertised in the Sears catalog.[57] The advertised 3-cord was apparently the same as 3-ply thread.
According to current industry conventions of nomenclature of yarns,
a cord is a yarn composed of plied rather than single strands; however, there is no logical way to produce a so-called 3-cord thread.
While 6-cord thread was made up of three plies of two single strands
each, a so-called 3-cord can only reasonably be composed of three
single strands making it, in actuality, a 3-ply thread. The "Conso"
brand of heavy duty mercerized cotton sewing thread labeled as
"three cord" I found to be 3-ply thread. Spools of "Twist De Luxe"
thread from the American Thread Co. labeled three cord also
proved to be 3-ply (see figure 4). Therefore, it is likely that other

Figure 2. Advertising trade card for Clark's O. N. T. showing top and
bottom labels. Card from the collection of Virginia Gunn.

Figure 3. Advertising trade card from Kerr & Co. showing spool of six-cord thread. Card from the collection of the author.

brands called 3-cord are also truly 3-ply. This should also hold true for the 2-cord basting thread advertised in the Sears catalog, which is assumed to be 2-ply as well.[58] Calling all plied threads "cord" appears to be more a result of an advertising ploy or the ignorance of copywriters than an accurate description of the construction.

This apparent confusion as to the nomenclature of thread goes back at least to the 1850s. An 1853 article in the *Scientific American* describes displays of spool cotton.[59] The display included cases which housed "three cord" thread manufactured by Jonas Ralph of England. Two cases showed products by Francis Hord of Manchester, one of which had "two cord" thread, the other "six cord" thread.[60] While the 2- and 3-cord threads described in the article are likely, in reality, plied threads, it may never be known whether the 6-cord thread was truly ply or cord construction.

The appearance of 3-cord thread in the Sears catalog corresponds to the appearance of mercerized thread.[61] Mercerization is a process of immersing cotton thread, under tension, in a solution of caustic soda. This process results in a stronger and more lustrous thread that also accepts dye more readily. Since 6-cord thread is tightly wound to obtain the desired fineness, it cannot be mercerized. The caustic soda solution cannot penetrate into the tightly wound strands. Three-ply thread has fewer strands than 6-cord and therefore is less tightly wound for the same thickness of thread. Consequently, 3-ply thread can be mercerized when 6-cord can not.

In the 1930s a quiltmaking resurgence occurred in this country, and by 1932 the Sears catalog offered a wide selection of quilt blocks, books, and other supplies to feed this new fad.[62] In 1934 the first quilting thread, Grandma Dexter's, became available through the Sears catalog. It is advertised as being a "strong smooth three cord cotton thread correctly sized. Mercerized finish."[63]

In 1960 Lily quilting thread is advertised as 4-cord.[64] While Lily brand quilting thread had been available through Sears since 1957, this is the first mention of it being 4-cord.[65] It is unknown whether the difference in the number of plies in the 1960s Lily brand quilting thread and the 1930s Grandma Dexter's quilting thread was a result of different brands with different construction methods, or if it reflects a change in the industry standard in the manufacturing technique of quilting thread. Yet, examples of recent quilting threads

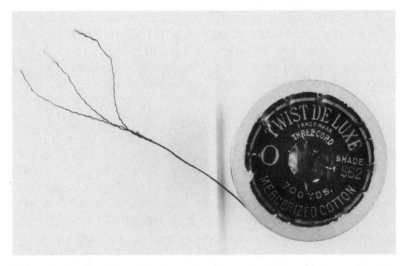

Figure 4. Spool of Twist De Luxe thread marked three cord wound with 3-ply thread. Collection of the author.

in my possession are either 2-ply cotton/polyester blend or 3-ply all-cotton thread. Other examples of quilting thread I analyzed also proved to be 3-ply cotton thread. One example is probably pre-1950s J & P Coats thread on a wooden spool; the other is a post-1960s Talon brand (a subsidiary of Coats and Clark) on a styrofoam spool.[66] This suggests that quilting thread has not changed much since 1934.

Thread construction was not the only thing to change; materials used to make thread also changed. Sears offered an artificial silk (rayon) embroidery thread for sale in 1924, but not an artificial silk sewing thread, probably because it would be too weak for machine sewing. During World War II, nylon thread became available through the Sears catalogs.[67] DuPont had first introduced nylon darning and sewing thread to the market in 1941.[68] While duPont's entire production of nylon was supposedly allocated for war-time production, nylon sewing thread remains listed (and presumably available) in the Sears catalogs throughout World War II.[69] Dacron (polyester) fabrics and thread became available in 1952, but it was not until 1958 that Dacron thread was sold in the Sears catalog.[70] Spools of Dacron thread that I have examined have labels from both Coats & Clark and from J & P Coats, showing that Dacron thread became available through J & P Coats prior to the 1952 name merger of J & P Coats and Clark Thread Co. into Coats & Clark. In 1969 Sears offered, for the first time, a cotton-wrapped polyester core thread which is available even today.[71]

Conclusions

Quilting and sewing thread analysis provides useful clues for helping to confirm the date of historic textiles. It must be remembered, however, that the type of thread present in an item is only an indicator that the item was made sometime after the thread type was first introduced. For example, textiles with 3-ply cotton thread would have been made after 1800; those with 6-cord thread would have been made after 1850; and the presence of polyester thread means it has to have been made after 1952. Furthermore, it is known that homespun thread was made prior to 1800 and again in the South during the Civil War. So, the presence of homespun thread is not proof of a late-1700s or early-1800s date for a textile sewn with it, but it supports such an attribution. The presence of linen or silk threads cannot be used as proof of an item's age either. Both types of thread were available through the Sears catalog well into the twentieth century. Linen thread was available until 1942 in the Sears catalog.[72] Silk thread is available even today in some fabric stores. It is important to examine a variety of clues including style, printed patterns (when present), fiber content, and dyes in addition to sewing thread, before assigning a probable date of manufacture for an item.

Acknowledgments

This paper would not have been possible without the encouragement, guidance and support of Dr. Patricia Crews, Director of the International Quilt Study Center and Professor in the Department Textiles, Clothing and Design at the University of Nebraska, Lincoln, Nebraska. I would also like to thank the Lincoln Quilters Guild for the 1996 Research Scholarship which helped to underwrite the research costs. The staff of the Historical Society of North Dakota deserves my thanks, especially Todd Strand for preparing the photographs and the entire Museum Division staff for their general support during the final phase of this project.

Notes and References

1. Theodore Raph, *Songs We Sang, The American Song Treasury: 100 Favorites* (New York: Dover Publications, Inc., 1986), 131–33; Vance Randolph in *Ozark Folksongs* (Columbia: State Historical Society of Missouri, 1949), 368–69; John Harrington Cox, "Singing Games," in *Southern Folklore Quarterly* 6, no. 4 (1942): 246–47. I had hoped the obscure reference to a spool of thread in this song could provide a clue to the origins of spooled thread. The origins of "Pop Goes the Weasel" are English, though it is unknown exactly when or where it was first sung. The earliest versions were popular as a child's singing game around 1620 and probably referred to a hank of thread, as did one version reported by Vance Randolph. Randolph's version has likely survived from the days prior to the introduction of spooled thread. Another interesting point is that different versions of the song have the price for the thread range from a penny to a nickel. A version reported by John Harrington Cox places the price at "six per cent for a spool of thread."

2. Barbara Brackman, *Clues in the Calico: A Guide to Identifying and Dating Antique Quilts* (McLean, VA: EPM Publications, Inc., 1989), 50.

3. Grace Rogers Cooper, *Thirteen-Star Flags: Keys to Identification* (Washington DC: Smithsonian Institution Press, 1973); Grace Rogers Cooper, *The Copp Family Textiles* (Washington DC: Smithsonian Institution Press, 1971).

4. Jennifer Faulds Goldsborough, *Lavish Legacies: Baltimore Album and Related Quilts in the Collection of the Maryland Historical Society* (Baltimore: Maryland Historical Society, 1994), 1.

5. Cooper, *Thirteen-Star Flags,* 25.

6. Kax Wilson, *A History of Textiles* (Boulder: Westview Press, 1982), 200.

7. Cooper, *Thirteen-Star Flags,* 24.

8. George S. White, *Memoir of Samuel Slater, The Father of American Manufactures* (Philadelphia: n.p., 1836): 262–63; George S. Cole, *A Complete Dictionary of Dry Goods* (Chicago: W.B. Conkey Company, 1892), 353; William R. Bagnall, *The Textile Industries of the United States, Volume I* (Cambridge, MA: The Riverside Press, 1893); bound facsimile of original book, (Ann Arbor, MI: University Microfilms, 1968), 161; Edward Hugh Cameron, *Samuel Slater Father of American Manufactures* (Portland,

ME: The Bond Wheelwright Company, 1960), 68; and Cooper, *Copp*, 26.

9. Bagnall, 161.
10. White, 262.
11. White, 262–63.
12. John F. Schenck, Jr., *A Story of How Sewing Thread is Made*, 2nd. ed. (Shelby, NC: Lily Mills Company, 1937), 7.
13. Bagnall, 164.
14. Catherine Fennelly, *Textiles In New England, 1790–1840* (Sturbridge, MA: Old Sturbridge Inc., 1961), 22.
15. Schenck, 7.
16. Harry Ballam, *The Story of a Thread of Cotton* (Harmondsworth, Mddx., England: Penguin Books Ltd., n.d.), 14; Coats & Clark Inc., *The Basics of Hand and Machine Sewing* (Greenville, SC: Coats & Clark, Inc., Consumer and Education Department, 1995), 16; and George A. Clark, *A Thread Mill in Miniature. How and Where it is Made* (New York: Clark's O.N.T. Spool Cotton, 1880), ii. George A. Clark is the only author who attributes the invention of cotton thread to Peter Clark.
17. Cole, 354.
18. Edward Bains, *History of the Cotton Manufacture in Great Britain*, 2nd ed. (London, England: 1835); reprint, (New York: A.M. Kelley, 1966), 346 (page references are to reprint edition).
19. Ballam, 15; Cooper, *Thirteen-Star Flags*, 25.
20. The relationship between George A. Clark, who was the sole agent for Clark's O.N.T. in 1880, and George Aitken Clark, who co-founded the American Thread Company, is unknown, but it seems likely that George A. is the son of George Aitken Clark.
21. Ballam, 15; Cooper, *Thirteen-Star Flags*, 26.
22. Cole, 356; *A Story of Thread* (New York: The Educational Bureau of Coats and Clark Inc., n.d.), n.p.
23. Cooper, *Thirteen-Star Flags*, 25.
24. Coats and Clark, 16.
25. Ballam, 16; Coats and Clark, 16.
26. This quilt is a part of the private collection of Byron and Sara Dillow. The quilt is made up of alternating equilateral triangles of early indigo prints and plain white cotton. It is quilted with three types of thread: blue 2–ply cotton thread, white 2–ply cotton thread, and white 3–ply cotton thread. The 2–ply threads, both white and blue, have a loose and varied twist and an uneven thickness along their length. This unevenness is suggestive of handmade (or homespun) thread. The 3–ply thread has a tight, even twist and is easily distinguished from the 2–ply discussed above. It is clearly a machine-made thread. These clues suggest an early 1800s date for the construction of this quilt.
27. Brackman, 50.

28. Cooper, *Copp*, 27.
29. Parthenia Antoinette Hague, *A Blockaded Family* (Boston, MA: Houghton, Mifflin and Co., 1888); reprint, (Lincoln: Bison Books, University of Nebraska Press, 1991), 55 (page references are to reprint edition).
30. Bagnall, 163.
31. Bains, 346.
32. Hague, 54–55.
33. Cooper, *Thirteen-Star Flags*, 25.
34. Ballam, 16.
35. Cooper, *Thirteen-Star Flags*, 44–47.
36. Grace Rogers Cooper, *The Sewing Machine: Its Invention and Development* (Washington DC: Smithsonian Institution Press, 1976), 63–64.
37. Cooper, *Thirteen-Star Flags*, 44–47; Ballam, 16; Coats and Clark, 16.
38. Cooper, *Thirteen-Star Flags*, 25.
39. Ibid.
40. Ibid.; Clark, 1.
41. Clark, ii.
42. Ibid., 1.
43. "Fair of the American Institute," *Scientific American* 6, no.7 (2 November 1850): 50.
44. Quilts numbered 1997.007.023, dated 1851; 1997.007.149, dated 1852; 1997.007.570, dated 1853; 1997.007.666, dated 1851 to 1853; 1997.007.697, dated 1843; 1997.007.730, dated 1858; 1997.007.774, dated 1854; 1997.007.859, dated 1859; 1997.007.876, dated 1841; James Collection. The threads were analyzed independently by Dr. Patricia Crews, Director of the International Quilt Study Center, and myself. In all cases, we agreed in our analysis that these quilts did contain 6–cord thread, not 6–ply thread, as was previously expected in quilts of this age. These expectations were based on the published research by Grace Rogers Cooper, cited by Barbara Brackman in *Clues in the Calico*. Artifact analysis confirmed suggestions that 6–cord thread was available prior to 1860. Current research is indicating a ca. 1850 date for the introduction of the 6–cord thread.
45. *Scientific American* (2 November 1850):50.
46. Cooper, *Thirteen-Star Flags*, 43.
47. Quilt number 1997.007.149, James Collection.
48. Cooper, *Thirteen-Star Flags*, 44, 46. A flag designated as A-1 has 2/2 cotton while other flags are described as having 4–ply thread. Cooper was inconsistent with how thread construction was designated. In the case of 6–cord thread, she sometimes referred to it as 3/2 s-twist cotton (p. 52, fig. 25) while other times she referred to it as 3/2 cabled cotton (p. 46). Therefore it is reasonable to assume that her reference to 2/2 cotton is a reference to 4–cord thread.

49. Quilts numbered 1997.007.479, dated 1844; 1997.007.481, ca. 1840; 1997.007.541, dated 1912; 1997.007.654, dated 1854; 1997.007.665, dated 1853; 1997.007.778, ca.1850 and 1997.007.859, dated 1859, James Collection. Each of these quilts contains 4–cord thread either as sewing, quilting, or basting thread.
50. *Fall/Winter 1962–1963 Sears Catalog* (Chicago: Sears, Roebuck and Company, 1962), 319.
51. Debbi Fuller, *Introduction to Sewing Trade Cards* (N.P.: Thimble Collectors International, 1988), 4.
52. Ibid., 5.
53. Ibid., 9.
54. Gordon L. Weil, *Sears, Roebuck, U.S.A.: The Great American Catalog Store and How it Grew* (New York: Stein and Day, 1977), 10.
55. *Fall/Winter 1896–1897 Sears Catalog* (Chicago: Sears, Roebuck and Company, 1896), 195.
56. *Spring/Summer 1972 Sears Catalog* (Chicago: Sears, Roebuck and Company, 1972).
57. *Spring/Summer 1905 Sears Catalog* (Chicago: Sears, Roebuck and Company, 1905), 850.
58. *Fall/Winter 1924–1925 Sears Catalog* (Chicago: Sears, Roebuck and Company, 1924), 465.
59. "Cotton Thread - American and Foreign," *Scientific American* 9, no. 6 (22 October 1853): 46.
60. Ibid.
61. *Sears Catalog*, 850. In 1905, Sears begins to advertise "Klostersilk." It is described as a "mercerized thread," which is "as good as the best sewing silk and no more expensive than ordinary cotton."
62. *Spring/Summer 1932 Sears Catalog* (Chicago: Sears, Roebuck and Company, 1932), 190–93.
63. *Fall/Winter 1934–1935 Sears Catalog* (Chicago: Sears, Roebuck and Company, 1934), 268.
64. *Spring/Summer 1960 Sears Catalog* (Chicago: Sears, Roebuck and Company, 1960), 334.
65. *Spring/Summer 1957 Sears Catalog* (Chicago: Sears, Roebuck and Company, 1957), 226.
66. Though J & P Coats and the Clark Thread Company merged in 1896, the spool marked J & P Coats must have been manufactured prior to 1952 when these companies merged their names, becoming Coats & Clark.
67. *Spring/Summer 1942 Sears Catalog* (Chicago: Sears, Roebuck and Company, 1942), 490.
68. DuPont de Nemours & Co., *Milestones in the DuPont Company's Textile Fibers History*, 13th ed. (Wilmington, DE: E. I. duPont de Nemours & Co. (Inc.), 1980), 3.

69. Ibid., 3; and *Fall/Winter 1943–1944 Sears Catalog* (Chicago: Sears, Roebuck and Company, 1943), 690.
70. Ibid., 4; and *Fall/Winter 1958/1959 Sears Catalog* (Chicago: Sears, Roebuck and Company, 1958), 350.
71. *Fall/Winter 1969/1970 Sears Catalog* (Chicago: Sears, Roebuck and Company, 1969), 699.
72. *Spring/Summer 1942 Sears Catalog*, 490.

Appendix
Time Line of Sewing Thread

*ca.	1794	Hannah Slater "invents" 2-ply cotton sewing thread
*ca.	1800	3-ply cotton thread available
	1806	Clark invents cotton thread as a replacement for silk heddle thread
	1809	Almy and Brown advertise cotton sewing thread for sale in regional newspapers
	1812	Clark opens thread mill in Paisley, Scotland
	1815	Coats opens thread mill in Ferguslie, Scotland
ca.	1820	First cotton thread spooled by Peter Clark
*ca.	1830	2-ply and 4-ply (4-cord?) manufactured cotton thread available from Manchester England and Scotland
*ca.	1840	6-ply cotton thread is on the market; Clark and Coats send representatives to the U.S.
*ca.	1850	6-cord cotton thread is available
	1852	3-ply "machine twist" silk thread on the market
	1860	Clark's O.N.T. 6-cord thread on the market
	1866	George Aitken Clark and William Clark form the American Thread Company
	1896	J & P Coats absorbs Clark Thread Co. but each division still produces thread under its own name
	1905	Mercerized cotton thread advertised in the Sears catalog; 3-cord thread advertised for the first time in the Sears catalog
*	1924	"Artificial silk" embroidery thread (rayon) first offered in the Sears catalog
	1932	Quilt books, blocks and other quilting supplies are advertised in the Sears catalog
*	1934	First advertised quilt thread in the Sears catalog; described as 3-cord
*	1941	DuPont introduces nylon darning and sewing thread
	1942	Nylon thread available in the Sears catalog

*   1952   Dacron (polyester) home sewing thread introduced J & P Coats
               and Clark Thread Company combine names to form Coats and
               Clark Inc.
        1958   Coats and Clark Dacron (polyester) thread available in the
               Sears catalog
        1960   Quilting thread advertised as 4-cord in the Sears catalog for the
               first time
*   1963   Nylex thread (Zytel bonded nylon thread) available in the Sears
               catalog
        1966   6-cord thread is no longer advertised in the Sears catalog, only
               3-cord is sold
*   1969   Cotton-wrapped polyester core thread is available in the Sears
               catalog

* Asterisks indicate the introduction of a new thread type. Such events should
be helpful in the dating of quilts and textiles.

Authors and Editor

Tracy Barron grew up in Virginia, but now calls Massachusetts her home. She earned her B.A. in English and has a Master of Arts in Teaching. When she resumed her teaching career after taking time out to raise four children, she discovered quilt history. This led to a commitment to combine her love of quilts and English in her scholarly work. Tracy has previously published on Rachel Field's quilt imagery in *Uncoverings 1996.* 454 Cambridge Turnpike, Concord, MA, 01742.

Carol Elmore lives in Manhattan, Kansas, and serves as president of the Konza Prairie Quilt Guild and on the board of the Kansas Quilters' Organization. She is an appraiser certified by the American Quilter's Society and the Professional Association of Appraisers of Quilted Textiles. Carol holds both M.L.S. and J.D. degrees and is a Riley County law librarian and a reference librarian at Kansas State University. 2412 Hillview Drive, Manhattan, KS 66502.

Ronnie Elmore earned his M.S. degree at the University of Missouri and his D.V.M. degree at the University of Illinois. He is the associate dean at the College of Veterinary Medicine, Kansas State University, Manhattan, Kansas. His career in veterinary medicine led to an avocational interest in pets belonging to presidents. He and his wife also share an enthusiasm for quilts related to presidents. 2412 Hillview Drive, Manhattan, KS 66502.

Judy Elsley was born and raised in England, but now lives in Utah where she is an associate professor of English at Weber State University. Her revised Ph.D. dissertation, *Quilts as Text(iles)*, Peter Land Press, and her book of essays, *Getting Comfortable,* Jumping Cholla Press, were both published in 1997. She also co-edited *Quilt Cul-*

ture: Tracing the Patterns issued by the University of Missouri Press in 1994. This is her third paper in *Uncoverings.* 2861 Marilyn Drive, Ogden, UT 84403.

Virginia Gunn, Ph.D., the editor of *Uncoverings,* served on the board of AQSG from 1985 to 1994. She is a professor of clothing, textiles, and interiors and the director of graduate studies for the School of Family and Consumer Sciences at the University of Akron in Ohio. Her research focuses on women's history and on nineteenth-century American textiles, costume, and decorative arts. 215 Schrank Hall, University of Akron, Akron, OH 44325-6103.

Heather Lenz holds a B.A. in art history and a B.F.A. in sculpture from the Honors College at Kent State University in Ohio. Her work has been exhibited at galleries in Ohio and New York City, and the *Interview Game,* her spoof on the critic-artist dialogue, is sold at museum shops across the country. Heather has received grants and scholarships to support her work in quilt research, art, and filmmaking. 879 Danmead Street, Akron, OH 44305.

Dorothy Osler earned a B.Sc. in geology from the University of Newcastle on Tyne and began work in museum curatorship. For twenty-five years she has combined lecturing, teaching, and writing about quilting with work as a freelance editor. Her research focuses on British quiltmaking history and she has published four quilting books including *Traditional British Quilts* (1994). She served on the British Quilters' Guild Executive Committee as the first Heritage Officer from 1983 to 1989. 1A Beaumont Terrace, Newcastle upon Tyne NE3 1AS, UK.

Jenny Yearous completed her first M.A. degree in anthropology and worked for ten years as an archaeologist. She earned her second M.A. in Museum Studies at the University of Nebraska and served as the first collections manager at the International Quilt Study Center. She is now curator of collections management at the State Historical Society of North Dakota. She is interested in helping small museums care for their textile collections. 205 West Interstate, #10, Bismarck, ND, 58501.

Index

Page numbers in **boldface** refer to illustrations.

In recognition of the very
generous support given by

Bill Garoutte

for sponsoring AQSG's 1998
Seminar Keynote Speaker
and for underwriting
Uncoverings 1998

In memory of

Sally Jeter Garoutte

Leader in quilt history research
and the founding of the
American Quilt Study Group

Paul D. Pilgrim
November 9, 1942 - November 12, 1996

A nationally recognized artist, teacher, designer, collector, and quiltmaker, Paul Pilgrim was born and raised in California. With Gerald E. Roy, he founded Pilgrim/Roy Antiques and Interiors in Oakland in 1969. Later, he helped establish the American Quilter's Society Quilt Appraisal Certification Program in Paducah, where he also served as interior designer for the AQS museum and curated several exhibits, including the national touring exhibit "Gatherings: America's Quilt Heritage."

His greatest gift may have been in the area of education. Throughout his life, he brought vitality to teaching. No matter what age the students, he made the subject fun. The same feeling is evident in the group of twenty-nine quilts he made at the end of his life from antique quilt blocks. In creating the quilts in mostly asymmetrical patterns, he caught the essence of making quilts for all time. One can never again gaze at a quilter's collage and not remember Paul Pilgrim.

Presented in his memory by
Gerald E. Roy
Pilgrim/Roy Antiques and Interiors

P B & TEXTILES

100% COTTON FABRICS
New Collections

NEW **BASICS**

FABRICS FROM THE
Oakland Museum
of California

Hills & Dales

Vintage

Summer Bouquet

NATURESCAPES
ANIMALS

Silhouette

Willowood

nine lives
& **old wives**

Italia

Baltimore Beauties®

color
spectrum

In loving memory of our family's quilting heritage,
the Pampe-Schleper Families honor

Lillian Elizabeth Emilie Frohbieter Bollinger
Born Evansville, Indiana August 31,1911
Died Bellevue, Washington February 19,1998
Member of the Valley Quilters Guild, Hemet, CA
and
Grace Marie Frohbieter Pampe
Born Evansville, Indiana January 10,1914
Died Evansville, Indiana March 23,1998
Volunteer for the Good Samaritan Home Auxiliary

Lillian was the prolific quilter and her sister Grace was the family's quilt protector. Each hoped future great- and great-great-grandchildren would know them best through their quilts.

The American Quilt Study Group is a nonprofit organization devoted to uncovering and disseminating the history of quilt-making as a significant part of American art and culture. AQSG encourages and supports research on quilts, quiltmaking, quilt-makers, and the textiles and materials of quilts. Membership and participation are open to all interested persons. For further information, contact the American Quilt Study Group, 35th & Holdrege Street, East Campus Loop, P.O. Box 4737, Lincoln, NE 68504-0737.

Phone: 402-472-5361
e-mail: aqsg@juno.com
http://catsis.weber.edu/aqsg